Irish History

A Captivating Guide to the History of Ireland

Free Bonus from Captivating History
(Available for a Limited time)

Hi History Lovers!

Now you have a chance to join our exclusive history list so you can get your first history ebook for free as well as discounts and a potential to get more history books for free! Simply visit the link below to join.

Captivatinghistory.com/ebook

Also, make sure to follow us on Facebook, Twitter and Youtube by searching for Captivating History.

Contents

Introduction

The history of Ireland (Éire, in Irish) is a story of centuries of conflict, division, and isolation. This can be felt even in the Irish myths and legends that speak about the first wars between the old settlers—the magical and mystical Tuatha Dé Danann—and the newcomers, the Celts who intended to create their permanent settlements on the island. Ireland is an island, geographically isolated from Europe, and at the same time, it represents the western European frontier. As such, the island was separated culturally, economically, and politically from the rest of the continent. At specific periods, even remote Ireland couldn't avoid the influence of major events in the world, such as the Roman Empire, the spread of Christianity, or both World Wars. But most of the time, Ireland was one of the last places to be affected by the ups and downs of the European civilizations. However, there are instances when Ireland happened to be the source of events of profound importance to the history of Europe. Irish monks, who spread across the continent first, brought Irish cultural influences and acted as one of the early messengers of Christianity.

But Ireland's proximity to Great Britain proved to be the most pivotal for the development of the events on the island. Since medieval times, the peoples of the two islands interacted; they fought, but they also exchanged cultures and shaped each other's nations. The political and cultural colonization of Ireland intensified during the 16th century and culminated in the 18th century when Ireland was absorbed into Great Britain. Profoundly different, the Irish fought back. They wanted to preserve their old ways, native culture, social system, and their own Brehon law. Most importantly, the Irish strived to preserve their separate ethnic identity. This identity was defined by very distinct traditions, language, and Catholicism—which, even though adopted in the 5th century, became the very foundation of Irish society.

At the end of the 18th century, the Irish managed to win various degrees of autonomy through political activities. After two centuries of long and bloody struggle, they became independent. For most of the struggle, the Irish were on the losing side, but they survived. In the end, they managed to secure the right to self-governance and self-identity. However, the country remains divided even today. Southern Ireland is a sovereign country, though with special ties to the north and Great Britain. Northern Ireland remains part of the United Kingdom, and as such, it thrives in a distinct way. But because it shares tradition, culture, and history with both the Republic of Ireland and the UK, the North takes special care to maintain its bonds with both these countries.

Ireland today is a prosperous place, its nation open to the world and at ease with the reality of shared heritage. English became the dominant language, but Irish Gaelic is highly cherished and has a vast and living presence on the island. Perhaps because of this bicultural heritage, Ireland has produced some of the best writers, painters, dancers, and musicians in the world. The whole world can now enjoy the traditional Irish Riverdance, read the great novels of James Joyce and Oscar Wilde, and listen to the ethereal voices of

Enya or Dolores O'Riordan (lead vocalist for the Cranberries). The end of the conflict in the North, as well as economic and social progress, have brought booming prosperity to Ireland, and the country continues to hurtle into the future. Attractive to many, Ireland became a haven for various immigrants and refugees. Today, many Westerners decide to settle on the Emerald Island, so often romanticized in the stories of old. The rapid jump Ireland made from being a country drowning in poverty and civil war to a modern, economically stable republic also makes it one of the most attractive places to live today.

Chapter 1 – The Early People of the Island

Lia Fái,l the coronation stone of the high kings at the Hill of Tara

https://en.wikipedia.org/wiki/List_of_High_Kings_of_Ireland#/media/
File:Lia_Fail.jpg

No solid proof confirms the existence of people in Ireland during the Paleolithic or Old Stone Age period. Approximately 20,000 to 15,000 years ago, the island is believed to have been uninhabited. The first people arrived somewhere between 7500 and 3300 BCE, during a period known as the Middle Stone Age. They were hunters, gatherers, and fishermen who came from the shores and coastlines of Wales, England, and Scotland. Scientists cannot agree on the way these first people traveled to Ireland. Today we know that England and Ireland used to be connected by land, but scientists continue to debate about the exact time the two landmasses split. It is possible that the first settlers of Ireland used this land connection to travel. However, it is also possible that Ireland was separated from England before even the existence of the first humans. In that case, the first settlers would have had to use vessels to cross the waters between the two islands. If they sailed, they probably crossed the Northern Canal, from Scotland to Ireland, first. Here, the two shores are so close that on a bright and sunny day, you can see the hills of Ireland across the water. Other settlers might have sailed on boats from the coast of northwestern England and Wales. The first settlements were raised along the coastline, where the people had easy access to the sea and fish. But they didn't limit their food source to only what the sea had to offer. They were also hunter-gatherers and ventured inland in search of game and forest edibles. From here, the first settlers of Ireland moved along the flows of rivers and streams to reach the inner lands of the island.

Very little is known about these first settlers of Ireland, and extensive archeological work continues. Still, the Mount Sandel Mesolithic excavation site in County Londonderry has given us insight into the life of the first people who inhabited Ireland. During the 1970s, archeologists found remnants of a settlement at this site, which radiocarbon dating placed somewhere between 7010 BCE and 6460 BCE. This makes it the oldest settlement found in

Ireland. It also predates any of the settlements found in Britain. The evidence found at Mount Sandel suggests that the houses built by these early people were round, made out of saplings that were bent inwards. These dwellings were covered with animal skins, and in the middle of each, there was a fireplace. The bones found around the fireplaces suggest what type of food they ate. Mostly they are the bones of fish, ducks, pigeons, and pigs, but the remains of eels were also found, as well as seashells. This excavation site also consists of scattered flint and various tools such as awls, scrapers, choppers, and chisels. There is not much evidence to cover the transition period between the early and late Mesolithic period, but the design of stone tools changed significantly. The people of Ireland started using bigger and heavier axes and heavier bores, which were radiocarbon dated between 6240 BCE and 3465 BCE. This is the period in which it is speculated that the land bridge between Britain and Ireland disappeared—if it ever existed. It is quite evident that several settlements were concentrated on the coastline, but it remains a mystery if there was any travel across the waters. From this period onwards, it becomes evident that the first settlers started moving to middle Ireland in greater numbers. Western sections of Munster were inhabited by this period, and significant evidence suggests that people's movements reached all the way to the end of the Dingle Peninsula.

The first people who settled in Ireland gradually spread all over the island. They even went further and inhabited the small islands around Ireland. They always made their settlements near water and woods so they could have easy access to the resources they used, but they were also always ready to move in search of new resources. They never founded larger towns or cities; they were divided into small groups of people, satisfied with their simple, nomadic way of life. But, around 3000 BCE, the first inhabitants of Ireland met new settlers, ones who came from afar and brought a new, revolutionary way of life—farming.

Strong evidence suggests that a new influx of settlers came to Ireland sometime after 3000 BCE. This is the start of the Neolithic period (the New Stone Age), and new technology was introduced to Ireland. The first farmers started tilling the soil, launching a more settled way of life. The production of food meant that there was no need to move to find resources. With their food growing out of the ground, people began rooting themselves in place, starting true villages. People in Ireland started clearing the forests to acquire the land needed for crop production. The wood they cut proved to be amazing building material that gave sturdiness and durability to a new type of house that started emerging during the Neolithic. Aside from houses, the people of Ireland used wood to produce furniture and fence the animals they started domesticating.

Neolithic farmers occupied the whole of Ireland, and we know about them thanks to rich excavation sites such as Lough Gur in County Limerick. These farmers were innovative and resourceful people who concluded that the soil was richer where elm trees grew. So, they built their settlements higher, on limestone deposits, avoiding the lowlands, which were rich with clay. They combined working the land with growing domestic animals. Wheat and barley were the most common crops, and during this Neolithic period, they started producing cheese. The Irish learned that moving their cattle to higher pastures during the summer would free the lower land for crops. In Ireland, this practice is called "booleying," but in common English, we call it transhumance. The houses of Neolithic Irish were built either round or square using peat, with a wooden frame, and some of the larger houses had a stone foundation. The houses were grouped in villages, and villages belonged to a wider community that represented a tribe. Tribes were not isolated. They often traded with each other, warred, or intermarried. The tools these early people used became even more sophisticated during the Neolithic: the axes were larger and shaped differently depending on their purpose, whether cutting wood or plowing the land. Drum-shaped spindles were found all over Ireland, evidence that they also mastered the art of weaving. At the same time, they started producing jewelry, stone, bone, and lignite bracelets and beads, with which they would adorn themselves.

The Neolithic period of Ireland's history also offers us first glimpses into the old religion of the island. Even today, we can observe some of the monolithic stone dwellings the early Irish constructed—not as their homes but as the resting place for their dead. Some of these dwellings were possibly used as temples where they worshiped their deities. The burial sites contain not only human remains but also jewelry, pots, weapons, and food-related items. We can only presume these items were left so the dead could use them in the afterlife. These tombs came in four different types: portal or dolmen tombs, court tombs (which are the simplest), wedge tombs (the oldest), and passage tombs (the most numerous). One of the most famous tombs discovered is the dolmen at Poulnabrone. It is unusually large and has a huge cap supported by several upright stone slabs. This tomb is dated to around 2500 BCE. But the most impressive tombs are the passage tombs, named as such because of the passage that leads to the main burial chamber. The passage tombs were the first monolithic buildings of Europe, and they are mostly concentrated in the midlands, especially in Boyne Valley. The whole structure of a passage tomb is covered in stone and earth, and they are often grouped in large cemeteries. Usually, the cemetery had one large tomb surrounded by a myriad of smaller ones. The most impressive and famous passage tomb is Newgrange (Irish: Dún Fhearghusa) in County Meath, built around 3200 BCE. This tomb is especially important to the early history of Ireland because it is the alleged burial place for the kings of Tara, sacred prehistoric kings. This was probably a ritualistic title, but it would reappear in the 9th century. Newgrange was also believed to be home to the Tuatha Dé Danann (the people of the goddess Danu), a mythical being who inhabited the island before the arrival of the Celts. The people of the goddess Danu were supernatural and possessed great powers and skills. However, according to Irish mythology, they retreated underground with the arrival of the (human) descendants of Noah, who survived the flood. The Tuatha Dé Danann continued to live and perform great magical deeds beyond the comprehension of the mortals; however, they devolved and became the little fairies and leprechauns of Irish legends. The myth continues, saying that the first humans who inhabited Ireland were known as Milesians because they were the sons of Mil (their ancestral parent), and when the Celts arrived in 500 BCE, they mixed to create the Gaelic Celts.

The great tombs of Ireland testify of a well-established, tribal society with a developed belief system. Some of the tombs are ornate, with carvings that symbolize the changing of the seasons. Some of them are devoted to the cult of the sun, while others are nothing more than ornamental lines and spirals. In the early tombs, human bones that were found were all burned, which suggests they practiced cremation. But that changed around 2000 to 1200 BCE, when the Irish started burying their dead without burning them. Each deceased was placed in a distinctive grave, often together with the items he possessed during life, as well as pottery specifically made for the burial. But historians don't yet know if this was a new group of people that reached Ireland and introduced their burial rites or if the old inhabitants of the island simply evolved their belief system.

With this evolution of the people's belief system came many changes, which are evident in archeological findings. The pottery transformed into beaker pottery typical of the Bronze Age. The urns buried together with the dead were now filled with food remains, and the deceased were buried together with jewelry made of bronze, faience beads, and amber. Faience was imported from the Near East, while amber was brought from the Baltics. It is evident that the Irish people started recognizing and using ores rather than stone. The first metalworkers came to Ireland around 2500 BCE, and they used natural sources of gold and copper, of which Ireland is rich. It is possible they exchanged the metals, raw or shaped into decorative pieces and tools, for the products of the Near East and other parts of Europe. They also mixed copper with tin, imported from Cornwall in England, to produce bronze. Because the bronze was stronger than copper or gold, these early inhabitants of the island started producing bronze tools and weapons, propelling themselves into the Bronze Age.

It was during the Bronze Age that the people of Ireland started building the *crannóg*, lake dwellings on artificially-made islands. This type of settlement would continue to exist well into the Middle Ages. But it wasn't until 1300 that significant changes to housing were introduced. Because of climate change, which brought much more rainfall to the island, the bogs started spreading. People were forced to raise their houses on trackways made of wood planks supported by piles. But it wasn't only the houses that were raised. People also built raised pathways to move easily across the bogs. For thousands of years, the Irish would continue to build such paths. Advances in farming and tool production came around the year 800 BCE. The agricultural innovation that changed the very foundation of farms was the introduction of ox-pulled plows. People no longer needed to spend their days working the soil with hand spades. The new plow sped up the process of crop growing and led to the increase of food supplies.

The first use of crude iron tools in Ireland occurred somewhere before 700 BCE, but it wasn't until the arrival of the Celts that the true Iron Age began. But the Celts didn't arrive in Ireland suddenly; they did so over a long period, estimated to be from 700 BCE to 100 BCE. The Celts came from Britain and continental Europe and carried superior weapons and tools with them, made of iron. But the Celts are not a distinct people—they were a group of Indo-European peoples who shared a similar language, culture, and way of life. This linguistic and cultural connection of the Celts is often disputed in the scientific community—and so is the direction of their spread through Europe. Nevertheless, they were the last people to arrive in Ireland, and they mixed with the old settlers to create who we today recognize as Gaelic Celts. It is possible that the first Celts came to the island in waves, as there is no evidence of violent invasion. Studying Irish myths and legends, as well as linguistic characteristics of the ethnic group, historians conclude that one of the first Celtic tribes to arrive in Ireland was the Fir Bolg. They are possibly purely mythological people, but they could also be connected to the Belgae people who lived in northern Gaul between the English Channel and the west bank of the River Rhine. We know the Belgae moved to England during the early Iron Age, and it is possible that a group of them, calling themselves Fir Bolg, arrived in Ireland. But this early history of the Celts in Britain and Ireland is highly speculative because the myths often mix with history. The Celts were prone to making up their history to connect ruling personas with divine and mythological beings. While the Fir Bolg settled in western Ireland, the northeast was settled by Priteni, or, as they are known in Ireland, the Cruthin. They are also a highly speculative group of people. There is written evidence of the Cruthin, but it dates from early medieval times and is untrustworthy. Early Irish monks used this name to refer to the early settlers of northeast Ireland, but also to the Picts of Scotland. The old Scottish name for the Picts was very similar: *Cruthen.* This is why some historians today believe that the northeastern Ireland settlers were indeed the Picts, a Celtic-speaking group of people who occupied eastern and northern Scotland.

These first Celts were a minority among the natives and had to use their skills to gain the trust of the people. They were probably traders and crafters, and because they brought much more durable and sturdier iron weapons and tools with them, they gained prestige. Soon, they used this prestige to wrestle power from local leaders and become the new chieftains of localized groups of peoples. By 150 BCE, the Celts were well established in Ireland. They brought with them a unique belief system and governmental institutions, some of which survive even today in modern Irish-speaking society. Social power structure certainly existed before the arrival of the Celts, but it was they who first established the political and social system of Ireland. From the gradual assimilation of the settled peoples and the Celts came forth the first Irish kings and heroes. The patterns of rule and life established by the emerging Gaelic Celts would last in Ireland until the arrival of the Normans in the 12th century.

The First Kings and the Emergence of Society

By the time Christianity took over Ireland, society was already well established. It consisted of different types of communities: clans, tribes, septs, and dynasties. Clans were groups of individuals united by kinship, descent, and the same surname. They always inhabited the same territory and were similar to the modern extended family. Clans were divided into septs, or subclans, if they were a part of a large clan. Numerous clans occupying one territory would form a tribe or a dynasty. The first emerging society was led by a chief or a king (*rí*), who ruled over a small agricultural and/or pastoral territory known in the Irish language as a *túath*. The king's word had to be obeyed within his realm, and to keep his position and his people happy, he had to be a strong leader capable of winning battles and leading raids. Violence and battles were constant. Even in peaceful times, human sacrifices were induced to please various deities. War prisoners were sacrificed to the god of war, while in particularly bad harvest seasons, a number of newborns were sacrificed to the god of the harvest. The extent of the violence that engulfed early Ireland can even be seen in the national dog, the Irish Wolfhound. Today this breed is only a distant memory of what its ancestors used to be. The Irish Wolfhound was used not only for hunting but also as a battle companion whose purpose was to pull down horsemen from their mounts.

At its earliest stage in Ireland, kingship was not hereditary. It was bestowed on powerful individuals who displayed exceptional leadership skills. But kingship also had a sacred quality, though not in all cases. Some kings were believed to be flawless humans married to the earth goddess. Such were the kings of Tara. The Hill of Tara is the place the Irish kings were inaugurated, and the sacred element of the kingship is closely related to this place. Its full name is *Teamhair na Rí*, which translates as "Sanctuary of the Kings." All kings had two main functions: to lead their people as warrior chieftain and to govern their territory through *fír flaithemon*, the "ruler's truth." The governance of the old Irish kings included setting the value of taxes and collecting them, maintaining law and order, organizing public works, and leading the people's assembly (*oénach*). These assemblies were held at least once a year and would gather the people from all over the kingdom to deal with tribal and clan matters. But these assemblies were also used as celebrations. Various feasts would take place, and people would marry or celebrate a victory over another kingdom. People would organize various games and horse races. Most importantly, during the assemblies, the laws were discussed or changed if needed, and deaths were recorded.

The kingship followed a strict hierarchy, and the high kings ruled over the petty kings. The later ones had to pay tribute to a greater lord. The Irish law established three separate levels of kingship: *rí túaithe*, the ruler of one small kingdom; *rúiri* or *rí túath*, ruler of several small kingdoms (overking); and *rí ruirech* or *rí cóicid*, ruler of many kingdoms (provincial overking).

However, it didn't take long for the provincial overkings to turn their territories into five different federations. They were called the Five Fifths, and we know them as Ulster, Connacht, Munster, Leinster, and Meath. Meath and Leinster would soon after merge together, forming the four provinces of Ireland that we know today. One more kingly title stands atop the Irish kingship pyramid: *Ard Rí na hÉireann*, or the High King of Ireland. However, this title seems to be mythological, as it always refers to a single ruler of pagan Ireland who unified the land. Today, it is believed that the title of the high king was invented in the 8th century CE to appease politically-fragmented Ireland. But in the 9th century CE, the title became a political reality. The provincial kings sought the title, and if one of them was proclaimed sacred King of Tara, he claimed the high kingship, too.

The whole history of Ireland before the 5th century CE is unrecorded. This means that historians must rely on archeological findings, as well as on myths, legends, and poems that were memorized and told by special individuals known as *seanachaidh*— the storytellers, or bards. The storytellers could memorize up to 300 stories and tell them to the next generations. However, this orally-transferred lore is prone to changes, as each storyteller could add or subtract information to create a narrative that would suit the current political situation in a kingdom. These early myths and legends were first written down in the form of a saga in the 9th century CE. Thanks to the oral tradition and the sagas, some of the Irish tales of old were preserved, and we have access to them today. One of the earliest mythological kings mentioned was Túathal Techtmar, who came back to Ireland from exile and defeated his enemies at Tara. There, he founded his splendid court and the traditional place of power for the kings who came after him. The first mentioned king who historians believe was an actual historical figure is Cormac mac Airt. He possibly ruled during the early or mid 3rd century CE, and it is said that a famous Irish hero, Fionn mac Cumhaill, lived at the same time. Myths and legends about these two characters are mixed with historical facts, but it is difficult to make a difference between the two. From the stories, we can conclude that during the reign of Cormac mac Airt, there was at least one armed force under the command of Fion mac Cumhaill. However, the deeds prescribed to these heroes are often magical: they allegedly defeated a fire-breathing fairy and Druids, pagan priests who were able to wield magical powers. But early Irish history is a period of superstition, legend, dreams, and rituals. The Druids did exist, and they worshiped nature in their sacred groves. They were the ones who performed sacrifices, most often of crops and animals and, to a lesser extent, humans.

While the kings and the assemblies were the central political institution of a kingdom, kinship played the same role for Gaelic society. This kinship was called *derbfine*, which can be loosely translated as "true kin." A *derbfine* was a group of individuals who shared a common male ancestor for four generations—a family, in a broad sense. The purpose of *derbfine* was to institutionalize property and inheritance. Land was the most important riches a family could own, and it was equally divided among its male members. Women had no right to own a property or inherit one, even if they had no brothers. In that case, the land would be divided between the male members of the wider family. Women could have an interest in their father's land, but only during his lifetime. Once he died, the land would pass only to the males of the *derbfine*. Equally, individuals had no personal rights in the eyes of the law. Everything was subjugated to the kinship, and only as a group could they truly enjoy their property. After the 3rd century CE, the kingship had a similar system of inheritance. All male members of the previous king's *derbfine* had the right to claim the crown. They could be the king's sons, brothers, nephews, cousins, and relatives. All they had to do was display leadership skills and pass various tests which would prove them worthy. These tests were ritualistic and included games, such as chariot rides, in which a candidate had to prove he was the best. But sometimes, it was enough for a druid to induce one person (not a candidate for kingship) into a sacred dream in which it would be revealed who among the candidates should be elected king.

In Gaelic society, the responsibility for exacting justice belonged to the *brehon*. These were scholars of the law, and they held the role of arbitrators in disputes. *Brehon* enjoyed high social status. Their law system was based on the code of *cin comhfhocuis,* which dictated that a community should be punished for a misdeed of one of their members. Therefore, if one member of the family broke the law, the whole family would pay for it. The payment could be made in money, livestock, or grain. The worst crime possible was the murder of one's kin. For this crime, the family could choose if they wanted payment or blood vengeance. The Brehon lawyers defined the division of Gaelic society as one kingdom. Society was thus made out of kings, lords, and commoners. Legal powers and rights were measured by one's social status. But the distinction between the lords and commoners was always fluid, as one could rise or fall in society, depending on his wealth and heroic deeds. This is why possessions were not truly a measure of one's nobility; it was the célsine, an institution of clientship. The nobles had men bound to them in servitude, but the benefits were mutual. While the lords possessed land, the commoners bound to him would work the land in return for payment. But commoners were not always bound to lords; they were free men and had legal rights. This means they could have possessed their own land, but they were also artists, priests, lawyers, physicians, musicians, crafters, etc. They had freedom of movement and were allowed to move between kingdoms. Complex subdivisions of the social classes existed, which were defined and maintained by the lawyers. For example, the chief poet, *ollam*, had the same status as a king but didn't share his power. Later, the same status was attached to Christian bishops.

Those who were not free were landless individuals bound to a lord through servitude. They could be workers, low-grade entertainers, serfs, and slaves. Slaves were prisoners of war or children of poor people who sold them into servitude. The social classes were differentiated from each other by the clothes and jewelry they wore. Men and women of higher social status wore a cloak, known as a *brat*, over the shirt. The cloak was secured with a beautiful brooch. They also wore other jewelry to distinguish themselves from the commoners. The higher social status one had, the more elaborate and colorful one's garments and jewelry. We know about the adornments of the high social classes because they were buried with their possessions. However, we know very little about the garments of the commoners because they were not buried with their possessions. The common folk were too poor to throw anything useful away. Nevertheless, we can presume commoners wore tight pants and a short jacket, a garment similar to the ones worn in central Europe. The opportunity for many Irishmen to grow and develop their wealth came with the establishment of trade with an empire that came to rule Britain—the Romans.

Roman Contacts

Under Julius Caesar, the Roman troops landed on the shores of Britain twice, in 55 BCE and 54 BCE, but they quickly left. The last time the Romans came to Britain was in 45 CE, and this time, they chose to stay. Romans conquered the British lands all the way to Scotland, and in the process, they built many fortifications. It is believed that during the Roman campaign in southern Scotland, under the leadership of general Gnaeus Julius Agricola, the Romans made their first contact with Ireland. Famous Roman historian Tacitus (56–120 CE) wrote that the people of Ireland were much like the people of Britain and that he came to such a conclusion due to well-established trade between the peoples. It is unknown if the Romans ever planned to conquer Ireland, but they never came to rule it. No archeological evidence attests to the presence of

Roman troops in Ireland. However, connections were clearly made, as many Roman objects dating from the first and second century CE were found in Ireland. They could have been acquired through trade or through raids on Roman bases across the water. This contact intensified during the 4th and 5th centuries as Roman power started to wane. The Celts took the opportunity and sailed to the shores of Britain to raid their army bases.

But when Roman rule in Britain ended in the 5th century CE, the Irish came to settle in Britain for the first time. The first large colony came from southern Ireland and settled in southern Wales. Others followed, settling in northern Wales and the southern shores of England. However, the most successful colony was that of Dal Riata, the Irish emigrants who founded their kingdom on the shores of northeastern Ireland and western Scotland across the North Channel. But back in Ireland, interaction with the Roman and British cultures brought many changes. The riches conquered in the raids on British shores caused a shift in the power balance among the Irish kings and chieftains. The colonies in Britain brought new resources to the dynasties back home, propelling their expansion. The Roman influence also had a significant impact on the language of Ireland, as we can notice that the earliest form of writing, the Gaelic *Ogham*, is likely based on the Latin alphabet—though some scholars suggest the Elder Futhark (rune scripture of Germanic peoples) or Greek alphabet. *Ogham* consists of twenty-five varieties of short lines and notches set at different angles on either side of a central rule. It was used first to inscribe on wood and other perishable materials, but it flourished during the 5th century when the people started using it to write on stone monoliths. *Ogham* scripture can be found all over Ireland and in some parts of Britain and Scotland.

Chapter 2 – Christianity in Ireland

Monastic huts at Skellig Michael (where Star Wars was filmed)

https://en.wikipedia.org/wiki/Skellig_Michael#/media/File:Skellig_hives.jpg

In Britain, the Irish first encountered Christianity. As the trade between the islands continued, as well as the exchange of the people, Christianity slowly found its way to Ireland. For historians, the most important aspect of Christianity is its practice of documenting everything. Thus, the first documentation of Irish history occurred in 431, when the new faith penetrated the island through its connection to Britain, where Christianity was also a very young and new religion. We consider the year 431 as the first year of documented history in Ireland because it is precisely recorded on a document that describes the arrival of the bishop to the Christians in Ireland. The new faith spread through Ireland very quickly and without causing any violence. Although we don't know exactly when and how Christianity first established itself in Ireland, Saint Patrick is the traditional central figure of the faith in Ireland, celebrated as a sole missionary who introduced Christianity and managed to spread it throughout Ireland. Saint Patrick left an elaborate story of his endeavor to bring Christianity to the people of the Emerald Island.

Christianity changed the way of life in Ireland as it brought forth a new institution: the church. Bishops were the leaders of the faith, and although the church as an organization arrived in the 5th century, monasteries would follow later, during the 7th and 8th centuries. The first monasteries in Ireland were simple religious communes that grew around more important churches. They included men, women, and children and resembled villages surrounding a religious institution. But from these communities came monasteries as we know them today, transforming from villages into sacred places of learning and faith. The monks of these early monasteries would go out into the world to spread learning and Christianity. They traveled as far as the continent to spread literacy, and the work of Irish monks is noted in post-Roman Europe.

The literature and scholarship spread through post-Roman Europe were maintained and cherished in Ireland. Monasteries became educational centers as well as centers of artistic expression. From the 6th to 12th centuries, Irish monasteries fostered a cultural golden age. They produced beautiful manuscripts and sacred objects made of precious metals and stones. But monasteries soon became economic centers, too, playing the role that would later belong to towns and cities. But at the early stages, society was predominantly rural, ruled by kings and petty kings by the laws imposed by the church. Soon the kingdoms merged into the four provinces of Ireland, and conflicts started on a larger scale. Internal dynastic rivalries continued between the kingdoms, and war was an omnipresent reality that lasted until the arrival of the Normans, who presented the Irish with a new, common enemy.

Saint Patrick and the Beginning of Christianity in Ireland

It is believed that Christianity first penetrated Britain and Ireland from Gaul, which already had an established institution of the church in the 4th century. The document mentioned earlier, dated 431, was written by Prosper Tiro of Aquitaine. In it, he describes how Pope Celestine I (r. 422–432) sent an individual named Palladius to become bishop of the Irish Christians. This document tells us Christianity arrived on the island before Saint Patrick started his work, but in the eyes of the Irish people, this saint is considered the father of the faith. This is probably because Saint Patrick's writings are preserved. In his writings, he mentioned visiting pagan places where Christianity had not yet reached. Thus, he painted the picture of Christianizing a pagan Ireland. Saint Patrick certainly gained many followers among the Irish, but the spread of Christianity wasn't difficult because the old pagan religion allowed for belief in miracles, on which Christianity is also based. However, the new faith had to adapt to the pagan mindset of the people, and it absorbed some of the characteristics of the old religion. The conversion of the Irish from their pagan faith to Christianity was smooth and non-violent. Ireland is the only European country in which there was no conflict between Christianity and paganism, and so, Ireland never produced martyrs.

It is impossible to say precisely when Saint Patrick lived, but it is known he worked during the second half of the 5th century. There is no historical source that documents his life, but Patrick did write about himself, although not much. Nevertheless, the bits and pieces are enough to construct a basic picture of Saint Patrick's life. He wrote two works: *Confession* (his spiritual biography and the account of his mission in Ireland) and *Letter to the Soldiers of Coroticus* (in which he complains about the enslavement of his converters). Patrick was born the son of a deacon in the Romano-British village of Bannavem Taburniae. When he was 16 years old, Irish raiders captured and took him to work as their shepherd. After six years of enslavement, Patrick managed to escape and reach his old home. However, he didn't linger there, as he had a vision that told him the Irish people needed him. Patrick went to Gaul to receive training as a priest and set for Ireland to become a bishop. Tradition tells us the year was 432, but this date cannot be historically confirmed. As soon as he stepped on Irish soil for the second time, Patrick started his mission. Over the years, he converted thousands—from kings, lords, and commoners to sacred bards and pagan priests. Many legends were attached to the works of Saint Patrick. The most famous is that he drove out the snakes from the island. But this is not a literal story; it's an allegory. Postglacial Ireland was already free of snakes, and the snakes that Saint Patrick drove off are a metaphor for Satan from the biblical story about Adam and Eve. But the serpent was also a symbol often used by Druids, and the story of Saint Patrick and the snakes can be understood as his dealing with the ancient pagan religion.

By the 8th century, Saint Patrick became the patron saint of Ireland, although he was never officially canonized because he lived and worked before the modern laws of the Christian church. Nevertheless, both Catholic and Orthodox Churches recognize him as a saint and even put him on the same pedestal as the apostles. Saint Patrick used his skills of persuasion to convert the people. He was aware that pagan customs were deeply rooted in people's consciousness, and he never sought to change them. Instead, he changed their belief system. That way, the social structure of Ireland remained intact even though a significant religious and cultural change was happening all around them. But there is one social aspect Patrick sought to eradicate: slavery. He was the first individual in Western history to advocate against slavery. The traditional date of Saint Patrick's death is March 17, and even today, this date is celebrated as Saint Patrick's Day.

The Irish didn't have red martyrdom (martyrdom due to violent death), but they did come up with their unique supplement of sanctity. The monks of the 5th and 6th century left the comforts of their monasteries and traveled to wild and rarely habited places where they would pray and seek inspiration directly from God. They would often die in the wilderness, outside of their kingdom's jurisdiction, and they found sanctity in what the Irish call "green martyrdom." Another unique aspect of Christianity in Ireland is the importance of monasteries. Unlike the rest of Europe, the most important churches in Ireland were led not by priests but by monks and bishops. This church organization was modeled on Roman administrative units established in Britain during the 5th century. The chief cleric of the monasteries was, at the same time, a bishop and an abbot. Ireland had two types of monasteries. The first resembled settlements and were economic, social, educational, and religious centers, often established near the main roads of a kingdom. The second type of monasteries were established deep in the forests, on the top of high cliffs, or in deserted places where nobody lived. These were monasteries founded by hermit monks who sought isolation from the world to get closer to God. One such monastery is Skellig Michael, founded anywhere between the 6th and 8th century, where modern movies, such as *Star Wars*, are filmed today.

The Irish monks had a unique appearance. While they dressed in the standard simple, undyed wool robes with a white underhood, the main difference was in their tonsure—the monks' practice of shaving their scalp as a symbol of their humility and devotion to God. The typical depiction of tonsure is that of a shaved crown. In Ireland, monks shaved the front half of their heads, from the forehead to the middle, leaving the back part to grow long. Monks' lives followed a strict order of prayers, and they were set in canonized time frames. In between prayers, monks worked to support themselves. They produced their own tools, plowed their own fields, grew gardens, and fished. Some monasteries even adopted an uncommon canon wherein the monks were required to pray while working. But the central occupation of all monasteries was the copying of sacred manuscripts. Some Irish monks became famous for their skills and artistic talents because, while the text was strictly copied, monks had the artistic freedom to decorate their work as they wished.

Society of Early Christian Ireland

During the early period of Christianity, Ireland didn't have cities, and it was the monasteries that served as not only ecclesiastical but also social centers. Monasteries were governed by rich and politically powerful clerical aristocrats, and some even became the residences of the kings. Such was Armagh, where the Uí Néill dynasty maintained its home. Armagh claimed it was founded by none other than Saint Patrick. Because of this, the monastery was granted a large piece of land by the chieftain Daire. (He also helped build a stone church which, during the 7th century, became the most important ecclesiastical center of Ireland.) In time, Armagh was given jurisdiction over all Ireland's religious matters. During the 7th century, Armagh ceased being a monastery, and its abbot-bishop was turned into a bishop only. During the 7th and 8th centuries, dioceses started forming, and they often took the shape of already existing kingdoms. Bishops were based in monasteries, but they started building their power and founded independent churches from which they could preach to the people. There were different types of churches—free ones that stood separate from the monastery and were not obliged to pay taxes to kings or landowners, and others that were attached to a kingdom, monastery, or wealthy family to whom they paid taxes. The most numerous were small churches, both free and unfree, scattered around Ireland to serve all the people.

From the 7th until the 9th century, Ireland had around three million inhabitants, but only about half a million to a million lived in the vicinity of the churches. Life in early Christian Ireland was rural, and most families lived in small isolated farms whose size depended on the family's wealth. Between the farms were large portions of wilderness, usually forests and bogs. Consequently, families rarely had contact with each other. However, the rural economy of early Christian Ireland demanded the existence of places where trade could occur. Since there were no villages or towns yet, monasteries took on the role of trade centers, too. They were usually concentrated in the lowlands and were surrounded by a significant number of farms. The farmers grew oats, barley, wheat, and rye, which they took to monasteries to sell or exchange for other products. Oats were the staple food of the Irish people until the 19th century, eaten in the form of a crude gruel. There were few vegetables and almost no fruit except wild apples. However, berries and nuts were abundant in Ireland, and because of their highly nutritious qualities, they were extremely valued. Irish also kept cattle, and milk and dairy products were commonly consumed. Women took care of the cows and milked them to produce cheese and butter. Sheep were mainly kept for their wool, but poor families consumed mostly sheep's milk. Although Ireland had a lot of cattle in that period, only well-to-do families ate their meat. Cattle, in general, were too valuable and were not slaughtered.

People depended on what they produced, so only a small part could be sold. Many families couldn't spare anything from their harvest for trade, and they felt extreme hardship if the harvest was low or if it failed. This is why famines, diseases, and social disorders, as the people blamed the government for their woes, were numerous. The people often migrated in search of better lives. But even if the harvest was plentiful, it did not guarantee a better quality of life. From the second half of the 7th until the 9th century, Ireland was often struck by various epidemics, which decimated its population. Religion played a major role in bringing solace, but many people chose to turn to old pagan gods and rites in search of a cure. Thus, the traditions and oral transmission of this old Celtic heritage lived side by side with Christianity. Religious and secular rulers enacted their laws and avoided social disaster by keeping the peace. However, Ireland's secular rulers cared little about peace when it came to relations between themselves. War and violence were common as each kingdom sought to expand its territory and claim more farms to secure its existence.

Early Kingdoms of Ireland

The top position of Irish secular society belonged to the kings. Early Ireland had many small kingdoms, perhaps even one hundred of them. But they were not all of equal status. There were small, petty kings who served under lesser overlords who, in turn, served the high kings. The pagan aspects of the kingship remained even when Christianity became the main religion of the island. For example, kings were still ceremonially crowned in marriage with the earth goddess. This marriage was sacred as it was supposed to bring prosperity both to the land and to the people. By the second half of the 7th century, the structure of kingship changed, and petty kings and lesser overlords started dying out. The 8th-century annals tell stories of how great kings defeated the lesser ones in battles and took their territories. But the petty kings did not completely die out; they transformed into nobility who were dependent on their rulers.

During the 7th century, in Ulster and Meath, the Uí Néill dynasty rose to power and dominated the midlands and the northwest. The rulers of this dynasty claimed the most prestigious Irish title: they proclaimed themselves "Kings of Tara," thus claiming supreme power over all of Ireland. The date of the Uí Néil's split is unknown, but at one point, the dynasty had representatives ruling over the southern and northern parts of Ireland. The southern family split again, this time into many smaller branches. One of them was the powerful Clann Cholmáin, who ruled the lands of Meath. However, their power veined during the first half of the 8th century, and the Síl nÁeda Sláine emerged as the dominant dynasty. By the 9th century, it was their king who claimed the overlordship of Ireland. The northern Uí Néillsplit into two branches: the Cenél Conaill in Donegal and Cenél nEógain in Derry. During the 7th century, these two wings of the same dynasty fought for prevalence, and at the end of the 8th century, the latter emerged as dominant.

In present-day counties Louth and Monaghan, three different kings formed a confederacy of nine individual kingdoms. They are known as the Three Collas: Colla Uais—the Noble, Colla de Chroich (Colla of the two territories), and Colla Meann—the Famous. The kingdom that occupied the shores of Antrim County and western Scotland was called Dál Riata. It was a powerful kingdom during the 6th and 7thc centuries, but British raids and conquests utterly destroyed it by the 11th century. The Uí Dúnlainge dynasty ruled the territories of Leinster province. They had their power base in the Liffey River valley and from there expanded, expelling other smaller kings to the fringes of the province. Ireland's southern province of Munster was ruled by the Eóganacht dynasty from the 7th until the 10th century. This dynasty was very close to the church, and one of its kings, Feidlimid mac Crimthainn, ruled as both a secular king and a bishop. He was a ruthless king who ruled between 820 and 846. During his entire reign, Crimthainn raided the territories of the Uí Néill dynasty and pillaged their monasteries. However, his dynasty suddenly fell down from grace during the 10th century and was replaced by the Dál Cais. The two ruling dynasties of Connacht were Uí Fiachrach and Uí Briúin, and they both claimed to be related to the Uí Néill. By the 8th century, Uí Briúin became the dominant one in the region, suppressing the other dynasty into oblivion.

During these early days of Christian Ireland, there was no such thing as a high king who ruled the whole island. The concept of a high king was promulgated by the learned monks, who wanted to implement the idea of unity into the minds of the kings and the people. The monks created myths that spoke of individuals who held all of Ireland under their rule. As the Uí Néill was the strongest dynasty and a major patron of the clergy, it was put forth as the main candidate for the high kingship. The political unity of Ireland was supposed to happen under their rule, and so the myth of legendary Niall, the founder of the dynasty, was born. Niall did exist, but many of his deeds were simply made up by the educated patrons of the dynasty. He ruled circa 405 and is remembered as Niall Nóigiallach (Niall of the Nine Hostages, as supposedly he took that many war prisoners). Niall's seven sons founded the seven dynasties of Ireland, but Uí Néill was the strongest and ruled the most territory. Naturally, they claimed overlordship in the large territories but were unable to take the title of high king for centuries. King Maíl Sechnaill mac Maéle Ruanaid, who ruled in the 9th century, was the first to be referred to as the high king in the Annals of Ulster, written from 431 until 1540. But Maíl Sechnaill's overlordship was constantly challenged by neighboring kings, and during his reign, he even had to deal with the first foreign invasion of Ireland.

Chapter 3 – The Vikings in Ireland

Ireland during the 900s

https://en.wikipedia.org/wiki/Early_Scandinavian_Dublin#/media/
File:Ireland900.png

The people of Ireland had not experienced any violent invasions. All migrations were peaceful until the end of the 8th century when the Vikings came. In general, the Irish Christians were left alone to cultivate their possessions and artistic treasures for centuries. When the Norwegians and the Danes arrived, they brought chaos as they raided mainly rich monasteries. However, the Viking invasions did bring something good to Ireland. The innovative new settlements—towns and cities—brought much better connections with the outside world. This was the first large-scale outside contact for Ireland, and it brought the opportunity of commerce unknown to the reigning dynasties. In time, the violent Vikings assimilated with the local population; they became Christians and learned the local language and customs. Initially, the Vikings settled only the coastal regions of the island, but they eventually ventured into the mainland to trade. Soon, they were drawn into the dynastic rivalries of the domestic peoples and started participating in native politics.

The Vikings also brought much more sophisticated technology and weaponry. By acquiring these, Irish kings were able to facilitate battles across much larger territories, with deadlier outcomes. The native royal dynasties were fewer in numbers, but they had resources and fought each other to expand their kingdoms. Because the stakes were higher, the battles became more intense, and it was during this period that the first claims of high kingship were made. In the end, it wasn't the Christian monks who persuaded the kings of the need for the political unity of Ireland. It was the common enemy, the Vikings.

The Viking Wars

Vikings first landed in Ireland in 795, and their first target was Lambay Island, just off the shores of County Dublin. Heavily armed warriors spilled from the bowels of their decorated ships and ransacked the monastic settlement, taking treasures and enslaving people. In the same year, the Vikings also attacked Rathlin Island,

Inishmurray, and Inishbofin. Their raids were always sudden a. quick, and they had no intention of lingering longer than was needed. However, the raids interrupted the golden age of Irish Christianity, and most of the artistically adorned Christian symbols were taken away by the Norsemen. The reasons the Vikings attacked the distant shores of Britain and Ireland remain unknown. They initially began raiding around the Baltic Sea and gradually spread from there to the west, east, and south. In time, they would reach Russian territories, Constantinople, and even the American continent. The Norsemen built the most technologically-advanced vessels Irish people had ever seen. They were built for speed and mobility, which explains their ability to successfully cross great naval distances.

The Vikings were still pagans, and they were surprised by the existence of the monasteries, settlements which held such treasures but mounted no defenses. Because Christianity came to Ireland peacefully, there was never really any need for the monks to learn how to defend themselves. This made them easy and perfect targets for the Vikings—the ultimate pirates of Europe. Hundreds of monks were killed in the raids, which happened again in 802 and 806. The first forty years of the 9th century saw increased numbers of raids on monasteries, but the Norsemen's tactic was always hit-and-run, as their main intention was to bring treasures home and not to linger on the shores of the new lands they discovered.

By 823, the Vikings had explored the entire Irish coastline. In 824, even the famous Skellig Michael was raided. The terror that Vikings brought to the shores of Ireland resulted in monasteries retreating inland, carrying with them all the treasures and relics they had managed to preserve. Kings of Ulster and Munster battled the Vikings as best as they could, but they couldn't match the speed of the Norse vessels.

inland proved fruitless, as the bands of the Vikings
1 the monks. Around 830, they dared to move to the
)f the monasteries. The first recorded Viking raid to
is in 836 when a band attacked the territories of the
.léill. But the next year was crucial because the
character of the raids changed. Sixty ships were sent on the river
Boyne and another sixty on the Liffey. This time, the targets weren't
only the monasteries. The Vikings raided and pillaged every
settlement they could find. They also sailed up the River Shannon
and the Erne and defeated every Irish king that dared to stand in
their way. In 841, the Norsemen set up their first bases in Ireland, at
Linn Duachaill and Dublin Hill. From there, they launched attacks
further inland. This was also the first time the Vikings wintered in
Ireland, and in Dublin, they had to build a stockade for their ships.
Completely unintentionally, they laid the foundations of the future
city.

In the first half of the 9th century, Ireland saw only the
Norsemen from Norway. However, starting in the 950s, the Danish
Vikings came, creating an even bloodier battlefield of the island.
The Norwegians fought the Danes, but they also fought the Irish.
The Irish also fought each other, as many kings saw the Viking raids
as an opportunity to grab more territory for themselves. But this
period was important for Irish history because, for the first time, the
Irish kings started forming alliances to fight the Vikings more
effectively. They even made progress, which can be measured in the
number of their battle victories and the fact that the frequency of
raids started dropping. In 845, the Irish king Mael Sechnaill mac
Maéle Runaid managed to capture and kill the leader of the Viking
forces. However, the Norse fleets continued to land on the Irish
shores between 845 and 860 before the raiding gradually stopped.
Although the Irish organized small alliances among themselves, they
never managed to unite against the Vikings as one nation. They
continued their dynastical fights, and the Norsemen proved more

than happy to jump in, siding with different kings depending on what they could get for themselves. The first alliances between the Irishmen and the Vikings were forged starting in 842, and from 850, there are more accounts confirming various such alliances.

During this period, the invading Vikings started settling in Ireland and sharing the land with the local population. Because they no longer had the intention of running back to their homeland, Scandinavia, they stopped raiding and started acquiring land, which they would farm and settle with their people. Needing to make alliances with the domestic dynasties, they joined local quarrels. During the second half of the 9th century, the Uí Néill kings built their main power base at Tara, and they tamed the Vikings who chose to settle in their territory. But most Norsemen settled in and around Dublin and made alliances with neighboring rulers to fight Uí Néill. The end of the 9th century was mostly peaceful, and no new raids or invasions were launched. However, this was just the calm before the storm. The second wave of the Viking invasion began in the second half of the 10th century and lasted for the next twenty-five years. A massive fleet of Viking ships gathered at Waterford Harbour in 914. The next year, they raided Munster and Leinster, pillaging monasteries, fortifications, and family farms. The Irish overking of the Uí Néill dynasty, Niall Glúndub mac Áedo, launched a counterattack and chased the Vikings through the territory of Munster during the year 917. However, he failed to drive them out of Ireland. He allied with Leinster but suffered a grave defeat. Two years later, he led another attack; this time, he planned to hit Dublin. But in this battle, the great Uí Néill met his end. Even though the Irish lost the battle, the Vikings did not continue raiding. Instead, they started consolidating their power in and around Dublin.

The Vikings had a tremendous influence on Irish society. They brought death and destruction, and many items of cultural heritage were lost, taken away from the island, and likely smelted away. While the death toll of the Viking raids was probably very high, life thrived and continued. Vikings did have some good impact on the Irish, too. They started settlements and introduced widespread commerce to mainly agricultural Ireland. When the Vikings eventually settled in Ireland, they turned from raiders into farmers, fishermen, and tradesmen. But while the Norsemen who invaded the British Isles and French territories settled inland, in Ireland, they preferred the coast, where they had first landed. They founded the first towns at Dublin, Waterford, Cork, and Limerick. These were all harbor settlements that offered a trade link to Britain, Scandinavia, and the rest of Europe. Dublin remained the main settlement for Scandinavians in Ireland, and it grew very quickly into one of the richest Viking settlements in Europe.

Trade was so important to Ireland that money was finally introduced in 953. That year, the first silver coins appeared in Ireland and were in continuous use until the Normans came. Together with changing commerce, the political and social life of the island changed, too. Expert traders, sailors, and shipbuilders were introduced, and they quickly found their place in Irish society. Overall, the social life of the people quickly returned to its familiar patterns after the deadly and gruesome Viking raids. Life returned to normal during the second half of the 10th century, and the kings continued to fight against other kings.

Dynastic Duels of the 10th Century

The second half of the 10th century was marked by dynastic struggles among the Irish kings. Already in 964, the leader of the Dál Cais (a petty kingdom in east Clare) captured the Rock of Cashel, the seat of the Eóganacht dynasty. Soon after, he sacked Limerick, a Viking settlement at the time. The ruler of Dál Cais, Mathgamain, proclaimed himself king of north Munster, but in 976, he was assassinated. His successor was his younger brother, Brian Bóruma, also known as Brian Boru. After avenging the death of his brother, Brian extended his kingdom. By 980, he controlled Limerick and all of Munster. He established his power base at Rock of Cashel, and from there, he launched attacks on his neighbors in the attempt to conquer their territories.

Brian Boru was able to extend his power because the Uí Néill, his neighbors in the north, were busy fighting their own inter dynastic struggles. High King Domnall Ua Néill (956-80) laid claim to the territories of southern Meath and even moved his troops there, but he achieved little. He was the last king of Uí Néill to hold the title of high king, as he was succeeded by Máel Sechnaill mac Domnaill of the Colmáin dynasty (although that dynasty was just another branch of the Uí Néill). Máel Sechnaill fought and defeated Olaf Cuaran, King of Dublin, in the Battle of Tara in 980, thus becoming the most powerful man in Northern Ireland. The first time he met Brian Boru was in the Kingdom of Ossory in 981, where he failed to contain him because Brian was able to coordinate his land and naval armies successfully. A year later, Brian launched an attack on Dublin but didn't take the city for himself. He requested a yearly tribute, which helped him finance his army. He continued his military expeditions in Connacht and Leinster, starting a conflict between Southern and Northern Ireland. Both sides fought for control of the whole island, but in the end, they reached a compromise. In 997, at Clonfert, all warring parties made a deal to divide the control of Ireland between southern and northern rulers.

Two years later, Leinster and its city Dublin revolted against Brian's rule, but the revolt also threatened the territories of Brian's old enemy, Máel Sechnaill. The two kings finally agreed to peace and an alliance to subdue Leinster. Their idea was to attack Dublin, which was ruled by Sigtrygg Silkbeard. But Sigtrygg didn't want to risk his city suffering a siege, so he took his army to meet the enemy in the field. Thus, in 999, the famous Battle of Glenmama occurred. The result was the defeat of Sigtrygg and the inevitable occupation of Dublin. Sigtrygg submitted to Brian, but Brian wanted reconciliation. In good faith, Brian married one of his own daughters to the ruler of Dublin, and in return, he married Sigtrygg's mother, Gormlaith ingen Murchada, the former wife of Máel Sechnaill. After divorcing his first wife, Máel Sechnaill had married Máel Muire, Sigtrygg's sister and the daughter of Gormlaith ingen Murchad.

In 1002, High King Máel Sechnaill failed to secure the support of all of Ireland's dynasties and was forced to give up high kingship. He was succeeded by Brian Boru, to whom he gave his support. But not all kingdoms pledged their allegiance to Brian, and although he was already in his 60s, he continued to wage war against those who defied his high kingship. Intending to rule all Ireland, he attached new meaning to the title of high king and proved that it wasn't merely a title. In 1005 and 1006, Brian completed a full circle around Ireland, fighting those who opposed him. After 1006, only Ulster remained unvanquished, and Brian was determined to defeat it. However, the northern kingdoms of Ulaid and Uí Néill were the most powerful ones of Ireland, and it took Brian considerable time and manpower to defeat them. Brian had the full support of the religious institutions by 1005, and they even named him Emperor of the Irish. By 1011/12, the kingdoms of Ulaid and Cenél Chonaill were no longer a threat to Brian's authority, but he left his sons to continue attacking them to keep them aware of what would happen if they rebelled. Brian held all of Ireland under his rule, but in 1013, Leinster and the Vikings of Dublin rebelled against him yet again. Brian sent his son Murchadh to deal with Leinster, who managed to lay a siege on Dublin. However, the city didn't fall until Brian joined the effort in April of 1014. The main battle occurred just north of the city, at Clontarf. This is the first great battle of Ireland's history that was recorded, and those manuscripts were preserved. Brian defeated his enemies, but he died as well, probably of wounds. He was already old but still energetic, and he personally took part in the fighting.

After the death of Brian Boru, Máel Sechnaill became high king again and held this title until he died in 1022. The changing political and social scene of Ireland was now evident even to the kings and nobles. The Vikings, once a threat that loomed over Ireland, were now integrated into everyday life. They melded with the domestic population, accepting the Irish language and customs. In the 11th century, the Norsemen settled completely in Ireland, converted to Christianity, and started marrying locals. They created a new generation known to history as "Hiberno-Norse" or "Norse–Gaels." But that doesn't mean the Vikings didn't bring their own influence to society. Some of the customs they brought from native Norway and Denmark took roots in Gaelic society, and although they were adopted, in nature, they remained Norse. The Vikings fought for the Irish kings and supplied the domestic army with broad shields, heavy longswords, and battle-axes. They also introduced swift cavalry to Ireland, taking battles to new levels of bloodshed.

The turn of the century and the Vikings brought a power shift in Irish kingship. The lesser kings were no longer able to protect their realms and were defeated easily by the stronger dynasties. The kingdoms grew as they absorbed the defeated ones. Some even grew to the size of an Irish province. The economy established by the Vikings, as well as the manpower, allowed the powerful overlords to acquire much greater degrees of control and authority in their territories. By the 12th century, only a handful of kings remained, while some dynasties completely disappeared from the political life of Ireland. As towns started developing, these kings abandoned their traditional power bases and moved to new, ever-growing settlements. The overthrown dynasties that managed to survive the cruelty of their conquerors turned into nobles. In time, they became loyal subjects to those who overthrew them. They also inhabited the towns and became representatives of an assembly of noble retainers, or *oireachtas* (the term still used for the Irish legislative body). These nobles, even though they didn't rule, retained much of their previous power. They built castles and were able to finance a standing army. In fact, the society of Ireland became militarized, and the battles were now longer, bloodier, and even more devastating. During the second half of the 12th century, the succession of kingship changed. Until then, it had always alternated between different branches of the same dynasties. But now, it became hereditary, inherited by the sons or any other male member of the family who carried the same surname. These ruling families intermarried but also fought each other all over Ireland.

The kings decreed the laws and imposed and collected taxes. The taxes were needed to fund the armies, and when these armies grew significantly during the 12th century, so did the taxes. The armies grew because, due to the disappearance of petty kings, the territories kings needed to conquer were larger. The kings issued their own coins and created a stable economy. They used money for the administrative expenses of their royal domains, and these domains were large. Constantly conquering and adding more territory to their kingdoms, the kings were unable to administer and govern it all from their power bases. Thus, royal officials emerged, often from the noble families that were once lesser-ruling dynasties. Royal officials were the feudal aristocracy, as they were tasked with heading the royal households, commanding the army and navy, and occupying the governor posts in towns or fortresses. They were awarded for their loyalty, as kings granted them large territories— often the size of minor kingdoms—to keep as their own. In return, royal officials expected military service as well as an occasional tribute. *Acallam na Senórach*, one of the most important medieval Irish literary texts, paints a very idealized picture of the kingship of the 11th and 12th centuries. In it, noble lords were described as utterly devoted to their kings, dying in battle willingly for the grace of their lords. In peaceful times, they all gathered in rich courts where they enjoyed feasts, plays, and fair ladies. But the reality was quite different. War, destruction, and death were everywhere, and they often went hand in hand with murder, deceit, and mayhem. The loyal nobles turned more treacherous, often changing alliances to suit their needs.

For the next fifty years following the death of Máel Sechnaill, nobody held the title of high king. There was too much uncertainty of war, as many kings grabbed the land of their lesser neighbors. Power shifted often, and there was not one individual capable of holding it all for himself. Military alliances were made and broken, and the whole period was marred by bloody murders, assassinations, burning of homesteads and churches, revenge, blood feuds, and even mutilations of enemies and their offspring. The key to winning the high kingship was to acquire as much land as possible, and the wars were long. Medieval records attached "king in opposition" to the rulers' names to emphasize that none of them won the submission of all other rulers of Ireland.

Brian Boru's sons were unable to grasp power after their father's death, but the dynasty didn't end. It prospered during the late 11th and early 12th centuries. One of Brian's descendants, Muirchertach O'Brien, was the most powerful king in Ireland during his reign (1101–1118). After his death, well until 1166, nobody was able to assume the same amount of power. O'Brien managed to secure control of Munster and Leinster after a long series of victories. In 1094, he killed the king of Meath and won the allegiance of Connacht, even though he had to deal with several rebellions in the region. O'Brien ruled as high king, but he was not opposed. In Ulster, Domnall Mac Lochlainn claimed the same title. But O'Brien is the first recorded king to marry his daughter to a foreigner, a British noble, thus securing his alliance and military help. He also appointed local rulers whose task was to govern parts of his realm that were too far off from his power base. Instead of giving them traditional castles to govern from, such as Kincora or Cashel, he ordered them to go to Limerick and Waterford, the towns previously fortified by the Vikings and therefore easier to defend. In the end, O'Brien was betrayed by his brother, who usurped the throne in 1114. Although O'Brien managed to retrieve the throne for a short period, he was convinced the prize was not worth the effort and retreated to a monastery.

In the west, a new king rose to power in the province of Connacht. His name was Turlough O'Connor (Toirdelbach Ua Conchobair, 1106–56), and he is considered the greatest warrior-king of the 12th century. This new king was on a quest to become the high king, and he surrounded Connacht with fortresses as a defense while he went out to take Munster and Meath, which he did between 1115 and 1131. He had no luck in Ulster, even though he tried numerous times to take it. In 1156, O'Connor died suddenly creating, a power vacuum that exploded in new wars for dominance in Ireland. He was succeeded by his son, Rory O'Connor (r. 1156–98), who proved to be unable to consolidate his power. During his reign, Rory had to fight endless wars with his neighbors, who saw him as a threat to the high kingship they wanted. Another king of the Uí Néill, Muirchertach Mac Lochlainn (r. 1156–66), proclaimed himself to be the high king, but this was not the end of the power struggles. History only repeated itself, and the events were very similar to those of O'Brian's reign. But Rory O'Connor continued to war for his right to the title, and in 1165 he took Meath and Dublin. The next year, Muirchertach died, and Rory became the high king. Ireland was now ruled by a stable and prosperous dynasty.

Just as it seemed that Ireland's power struggle was about to end and that feudal-based hereditary kingship would be established on the model of central and western European countries, the king of Leinster, MacMurrough, intervened to end the centralization of Ireland's rule. MacMurrough had been defeated by O'Connor, but he ruled a little province whose people were prone to rebellions. His kingdom was centered around Ferns in County Wexford. A private quarrel erupted between MacMurrough and another emerging dynasty, O'Rourke. MacMurrough abducted O'Rourke's wife, humiliating him in the process. O'Rourke waited twelve years for revenge, and the opportunity came in 1166 when MacMurrough was abandoned by some of his allies. He stood isolated, and it was the perfect opportunity to attack him. O'Rourke had help from the Norsemen of Wexford, and they managed to defeat MacMurrough and destroy his castle at Fern. But MacMurrough escaped to Dublin. Eventually, he was banished from Ireland by High King O'Connor and fled to Bristol, England. Then he continued to Normandy in France to find King Henry II (1133–89) and ask him for help. But little did he know that by doing so, he would invite the invasion of Ireland, an invasion which would change the Emerald Island forever.

Chapter 4 – The Norman Invasion

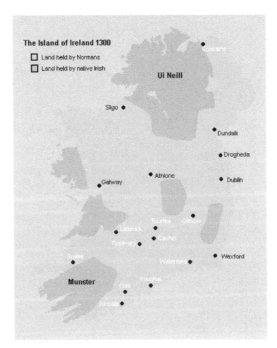

Norman possessions in Ireland in 1300s

The Normans came to Ireland in 1169, but they were in England 100 years earlier. The Norman invasion of the island is one of those history-making events, but certainly, their Irish contemporaries didn't see it like that. Normans brought their own political system, culture, and law and, with them, tied Ireland closer to the rest of Europe. Ireland became the Normans' possession and was governed from a distance from England. The Irish kings didn't quite disappear after the Normans came. They continued to rule as subjects of the English king, and their territories were significantly reduced. But the Normans never came in large enough numbers to take the whole island. Instead, they took the best land, and since they preferred to live inland, some coastal areas remained predominantly inhabited by the Irish population. The Normans, just like the Vikings before them, quickly became yet another layer of society and another player who came to wrestle over power and influence on the island.

In time, the Normans would mix with the Irish and create a subgroup of people, the "Anglo-Irish." They adapted to Gaelic customs and culture while acknowledging their English ruler. But they did demand a certain level of independence from England. Gaelic people, on the other hand—those who were purely Irish— demanded complete independence. As a third group inhabiting Ireland, the Normans sought to control the first two groups. By the end of the 14th century, England was so preoccupied with international events that it cared little about Ireland and ruled it only in name, allowing Ireland's local rulers to resume governance. But the monarchs in London would become interested in their possession of Ireland again in the 16th century and would start what is known as the English Reformation of Ireland, changing the political and social structure of the island.

The Normans Are Coming (1169-1175)

The idea of invading Ireland wasn't anything new to Henry II. As a ruler of the Angevin Empire that stretched from southern France to northern England, Henry contemplated acquiring Ireland, too. He even got permission from Pope Adrian IV (r. 1154-59), but the opportunity hadn't presented itself—until now. Henry received Dermot MacMurrough, took his offer of loyalty, and sent him off to England with gifts and invitation to all Englishmen to help the Irish cause. MacMurrough returned to Bristol and started recruiting the Normans of England, who were ever in search of land and wealth. They volunteered, as they saw Ireland as a perfect opportunity to gain personal wealth. MacMurrough also found a leader who could command the Normans across the sea, Richard FitzGilbert de Clare (ca. 1130-76), the second Earl of Pembroke. He was perfect because he had been battle-tested in Wales, where he continuously fought the resistance of local people to Norman rule. The Earl of Pembroke was also not married, and he didn't have Henry II's favor. He had nothing holding him in England, but he still proved to be a hard bargain. He demanded the hand of MacMurrough's eldest daughter in marriage and the succession right to Leinster.

The first Norman invasion arrived on the island in early May of 1169, near Bannow Bay. They numbered around 600 soldiers and knights in mail armor, carrying longswords and spears. Bolstered by a squadron of cavalry, they first defeated the Norsemen of Wexford. This was enough to convince O'Connor and O'Rourke to recognize MacMurrough as king of Leinster south of Dublin. In turn, the restored king recognized O'Connor as the High King of Ireland. But MacMurrough wanted to expand his territories, and he urged Richard FitzGilbert to come to his aid. Meanwhile, Henry II changed his mind about Ireland because he was insecure about the strength of his rule over the Angevin Empire, and he withdrew his consent. To make sure his orders were followed, Henry imposed an embargo on exporting goods to Ireland, but it was too late. The

Normans already had a taste of Ireland, and they wanted the land for themselves. On August 23, 1173, the Earl of Pembroke landed near Waterford with an army of 1,000 foot soldiers and 200 knights. The combined forces of MacMurrough and Pembroke took Waterford. They celebrated the marriage between the earl and the daughter of the king of Leinster and set out to take Dublin, as well. At this point, Dublin was an independent Hiberno-Norse kingdom. Pembroke ordered a surprise attack with a small band of raiders, which managed to penetrate the city's defenses. Dublin fell on September 21, 1170.

MacMurrough died in the early months of 1171, leaving the Earl of Pembroke to deal with the tribes of Leinster, which revolted against his succession. The earl also had to face the attacks of the deposed king of Dublin, who invited the Viking army of Norway to help him regain his kingdom. O'Connor, O'Rourke, and other native rulers of Ireland also attacked the Norman commander, taking advantage of his isolation. However, the Earl of Pembroke wouldn't give up so easily on his newly-acquired Irish possession. He was a determined warrior and managed to defeat all his enemies. But the success of Richard FitzGilbert in Ireland alarmed King Henry II, who feared that Pembroke would try to make an independent Norman kingdom out of Ireland. The defeated Irish also sent an invitation to Henry to come and help dispose of Pembroke, and on October 17, 1171, Henry II personally came to Ireland. He landed in Crook, near Waterfront, and brought with him a full army of knights, soldiers, cavalry, and archers. The Earl of Pembroke was subdued, and Richard FitzGilbert offered Leinster to Henry in fiefdom. Intimidated by the size of the royal army, other Irish rulers also offered their submission, homage, and tribute to the Angevin king. The only ones who didn't do so were Cenél nEógain and Cenél Conaill, dynasties that resided over the far north and were preoccupied with their own dynastic quarrels at the time. In 1172, Pope Alexander III (r. 1159–81) confirmed

Henry as "Lord of Ireland" and issued a proclamation to the Irish kings to accept Henry as their lord. The Irish bishops followed the example of the pope and urged local rulers to submit to their new lord. One by one, they followed, and the English kings kept the title "Lord of Ireland" until 1541.

Once Henry secured Ireland, he granted Dublin to his supporters from England. He continued to issue charters by which he granted land in Ireland to those who had helped him ascend the throne of England back in 1154. In this manner, he granted the whole province of Meath to one Hugh de Lacy to act as a counterbalance to the Earl of Pembroke's power in Leinster. He also appointed de Lacy as commissioner of Dublin, with the right to act as a justiciar, to recruit tenants for royal estates, and to represent the royal government in Ireland. On April 17, 1172, Henry sailed back to England and Normandy, where he needed to deal with the pressing matters of his kingdom. By 1175, the Normans had quelled all Irish rebellions that rose against their rule, and on October 6, 1175, Henry II signed the Treaty of Windsor with Rory O'Connor, acknowledging him as High King of Ireland with the right to collect Henry's tribute from lesser kings. But O'Connor was the high king, and he had the power over the territories outside Norman rule. In Leinster, Meath, Waterford, Dublin, and other places, he had no jurisdiction. Even in other regions, the ones inhabited with the Irish, O'Connor had little influence and was unable to enforce the treaty. His title had power only in the territory that he controlled in Connacht. The Normans were hungry for more lands, and they demanded it from Henry. In the end, the English king started granting it to his nobles without even consulting O'Connor or the previous rulers of those lands.

Henry quickly lost interest in Ireland, as he was pressed by the royal issues of other areas of his kingdom. He continued to keep the Norman nobles who lived in Ireland in check because he was afraid they would demand independence. But that didn't happen.

The invasion of the island continued as planned, and it was slow but steady. The Earl of Pembroke died in 1176, leaving as his successors only a boy (who would die soon) and an infant daughter. Because of this, the entire province of Leinster became the protectorate of the king. But Henry had no intentions of concerning himself with Ireland. He transferred the title "Lord of Ireland" to his son John (1167–1216), keeping only the cities of Cork and Limerick for the Crown. John visited Ireland for the first time as a young prince in 1185. He is remembered as being rude to the Irish kings who came to pay him homage. By giving the northeastern part of the kingdom of Limerick to Theobald Walter, first baron Butler, and to William de Burgh, John created two prominent Anglo-Irish dynasties—Butler and Burgh.

When John became king in 1199, he started granting Irish land, in smaller portions, to a large number of tenants-in-chief. Normans built fortresses in the areas they settled, usually near the bigger economic centers such as towns and abbeys. In the 1200s, the building material changed. Instead of wood, the Normans used stone to build their massive fortresses and castles, whose ruins can still be found across Ireland. But the Norman takeover of the island wasn't planned or centralized. The English kings were always too busy leading battles elsewhere, their attention drawn to Ireland only whenever greedy Norman lords became too powerful. When John Courcy, for example, moved his armies west across the Bann River to meddle in the affairs of the Irish rulers, King John acted. He disheartened him by granting some land Courcy's ambitious younger brother, Hughe de Lacy, Lord of Meath. In 1205, John even granted him the title of palatine Earl of Ulster. But when, in 1209, Lacy sheltered one of John's enemies, William de Braose, John decided to visit Ireland for the second time. In his anger, the king came with the army and marched on Ulster, capturing Carrickfergus and forcing de Lacy to flee. Meath and Ulster were declared the possession of the Crown.

The modern Irish government and political system owe their existence to the settlers from England and to King John, who set up the first Irish royal government. John's predecessor, King Henry II, and set up a justiciar—the chief representative of Ireland who relied on a council of feudal tenants-in-chief. But John and his successors transformed the council of tenants-in-chief to the King's Council in Ireland. The council was assisted by many permanent royal officials. In time, the council took the name "The Great Council," and during the 13th century, it consisted of barons and officials who held parliamentary sessions modeled after those of England. In 1204, King John ordered the construction of Dublin Castle, and when it was finished, it became the seat of the English government in Ireland. King John also introduced his coinage in Ireland and started collecting royal revenues. Over time, the liberties of landowners were diminished, and counties were established, each with its own legal apparatus. The county court for Dublin had appeared earlier, in the 1190s, but by 1260, seven more were in existence: Waterford, Kerry, Cork, Limerick, Tipperary, Louth, and Connacht. In 1297, they were joined by Kildare and in 1306 by Carlow.

The last native archbishop of Dublin was Saint Laurence O'Toole. After he died in 1180, all appointees were under royal control, which means they were of English origin. Since the newly-established governmental system of Ireland needed clerks trained to run it, the Crown appointed English staff taken from the English Church since education was largely limited to the clergy. All colonized parts of Ireland practice the same rule of appointing English religious leaders as servants of both the church and the state. The archbishops also held the office of chancellor, treasurer, or justiciar, depending on the individual abilities of the person elected. John's idea was to appoint Anglo-Normans as bishops of all Irish prelates, but Armagh resisted. For another century, they kept an Irish bishop, but after 1303, that was no longer the case. The

Norman clergy were different from the native Irish ones. They brought with them the reformed English church practices and the new monastic orders. The Norman lords were generous in granting them land, and the boundaries of diocesan in the colonies often coincided with those of the Norman lords' estates. But in the areas where the Irish people predominated and were in control, the size of dioceses varied greatly. Some were so huge that lord tenants (rich tenants who rented vast lands) paid rent to the bishopric. The Irish clergy kept the characteristics of their church alive, including clerical marriage and concubinage. Clerical offices were hereditary, and they often acted as patrons towards the bards and poets.

During the 13th century, relations between the native Irish (referred to as Gaelic Irish or Goidil) and the Normans were in constant status quo. Since the Irish kings ruled in accordance with the laws of the English kings and obeyed the royal institutions and crown justiciar, their reign was very long. The Normans didn't dare attack them, as they had the approval of the English king, but some power struggles did exist. Greedy lords always sought to grab more land, but they never did so to disrupt the status quo. When it did come to battle, the Irish relied on their numbers, as they still held a majority on the island, while the Normans had superior weapons and military tactics. (The Normans introduced the longbow and mail armor to Ireland.) However, soon the Norman lords realized the difficult Irish terrain was more suited to lighter armor. But the Irish kings started wearing mail, as it provided them with the necessary protection from Norman archers. The Norman effectiveness in battle is best displayed in the conquest of Connacht in 1235. But the power struggle around this province originated a decade earlier when Hubert de Burgh ran the government in Ireland. In 1226, he granted Connacht to Richard de Burgh, the son of his late brother, William de Burgh (also known as William the Conqueror). But the proud O'Connor kings also laid claim to this territory, and it was their representative, Rory O'Connor, who had recently become high king. They resisted the Normans, and a decade-long resistance was mounted. However, the Irish proved to be no match for the Normans, and by 1235, only the present-day counties of Leitrim and Roscommon remained under Irish rule. By 1250, the Normans held more than three-fourths of the island under their control. They held the best lands, plains, and coasts and left the boglands, steep hills, and forests to the Irish.

Gaelic Revival

Ireland still lacked organized leadership and control, and in the late 13th century, the Normans slackened their drive. They occupied the best land and farms in Leinster and Munster, but outside of that, they held only bits of territory here and there. The Normans were also few, and the mighty families were unable to spread because of the lack of male heirs willing to stay. They would often go to Wales, Scotland, or even the continent to fight wars for England. The Irish started growing not only in number but also in their opposition to the Normans. First to resist the Normans was the MacCarthy clan, as they were pinned down to the extreme southwest of the island. They fought against the FitzThomas branch of the Fitzgerald family that held the lands of north Kerry. The Irish leader was Finghim MacCarthy, and he defeated the FitzThomas troops in 1261 at the Battle of Callanan (in Kerry County). The Gaelic victory was so great that it secured MacCarthy's position of independent ruler of the territory for centuries to come. Similarly, when the Fitzgeralds began spreading to the northwest in 1270, the O'Donnell clan of Donegal stood in their way. The Irish quickly adapted their military forces, and now they were the equals of the Normans. They also started using Norse-Scottish mercenaries, known as the gallowglasses (from Irish *gall óglaigh*, the foreign warriors).

In the second half of the 13th century, the Irish tried to claim political unity by reviving the title of high kingship. But disagreements and old grudges still occurred, and when Brian O'Neill of Cenél nEógain claimed the title in 1258, he was disputed by his neighbor, O'Donnell of Donegal. Two years later, O'Brian died in battle against the local Normans. It is interesting that in 1262/3, the Irish offered the title of high king to an outsider. They needed all the help they could get to assert their dominion over their lands, so they offered the title to the king of Norway, Haakon IV (1204-1263). Haakon died before he landed in Ireland, but in 1315, the title was again offered to an outsider. This time, it was Edward Bruce (1280-1318), the brother of Scottish King Richard Bruce. In May of 1315, Edward landed in Ireland, leading an army of Scots, and he formed an alliance with Donal O'Neill, son of Brian. Edward's forces waged against the Anglo-Norman colonists for the next three years, but at the Battle of Faughart (County Louth), he was killed in 1318. His death marked the last attempt of the Irish to create a united kingdom, by which they hoped to expel the Normans from the island. The efforts to find a national leader died out, and the fact that the Irish survived the rest of the Middle Ages can be attributed to the local chieftains or confederations of chieftains.

Even though the Irish people's attempts to unite against the common enemy failed, they did manage to retrieve large parts of their territory. However, they failed to completely stop the Norman colonization. The settled lords of eastern Ireland moved to the west. They built new castles and divided the land among Norman barons, but they lacked the manpower, so most of the population of newly-acquired western territories remained Irish. The Irish agreed to work the land of the Norman lords, but no matter how hard they tried, the lords could not get the population to obey Norman laws. Instead, they chose to be obedient only to their local chieftains, who, in turn, paid tribute to the Norman lords. Because the

Normans and the Irish were forced to live together, some of the families built close relationships. They even started intermarrying and allying with each other against common enemies. They also feuded with each other. The result of these local quarrels was land swaps, and so one family would become superior to the other. In such a manner, the Burghs fought a feud with the Fitzgeralds between 1264 and 1296. The Burghs acquired so much territory that they ended up being lords of both Ulster and Connacht.

During the 14th century, the Normans domesticated in Ireland and were gradually becoming "Anglo-Irish." They had been in Ireland for generations now, and their interests in England had vanished. Once colonizers, they became locals, and they started building their society and political and judicial systems, which were modeled after the English pattern. The old assemblies that had started in the 11th century took the shape of a real parliament in 1297. A bicameral legislature emerged at the same time as in England, divided into the House of Lords and the House of Commons. The first was composed of bishops and aristocrats, while the second consisted of members elected from rural and urban representatives. The first Parliament of Ireland met in 1297 during the reign of King Edward I (r. 1272–1307). But King Edward never showed much interest in the island. He saw it as a source for men, money, and provisions for the army that he sent to wage wars in Scotland, France, or Wales. English institutions, whether they were political or judicial, never took hold in areas ruled by Gaelic lords. The cultural divide between the English and the Irish was vast. The Parliament of 1297 even brought measures legislating against the English adoption of Irish culture, habits, and customs. Use of the Gaelic language and Irish modes of dress, as well as moral standards such as trial marriages, the ease of divorce or sale, and the bartering of wives—all standard for Irish society—were forbidden to English residents.

In the early 14th century, the Irish Parliament granted growing powers to some of the Anglo-Irish families. The Parliament became a delegation of authority distant from the royal government in London and, therefore, out of its influence. These families acquired the titles of earls, and these titles gave them the right to seek even more power. John Butler (d.1337) was made the first Earl of Ormond in 1329. The two branches of the Fitzgerald family both acquired earldoms. In 1316, John FitzThomas Fitzgerald became Earl of Kildare, and in 1329, Maurice FitzThomas Fitzgerald became Earl of Desmond. Over time, these families acquired so much power that they were granted wide-ranging freedoms in their territories.

The stance King Edward I took on Ireland was continued by his successors Edward II (r. 1307–27) and Edward III (r. 1327–77). Ireland was drained of its resources and men, who were sent to fight foreign wars such as the Hundred Years' War (1337–1453), a very long war with France that almost bankrupted Ireland. During this war, the administration in Dublin was reduced to its bare minimum, as there were no men to spare to occupy the offices. Those who stayed were so corrupt and incompetent that they led the country to its very bottom. The government was led by the rich landlords, but they could not maintain effective rule. These magnates were driven by personal interests and would often make decisions that harmed their colony. Private wars between the families still tortured Ireland, and the Anglo-Irish would often employ Irish vassals to start local revolts and help their cause. Many of the great landowners decided to move out of Ireland. In fact, at the end of the reign of Edward II, more than half of the land in Ireland was possessed by absentee owners. That meant these estates were underdeveloped, and what little revenue they produced was drained away to England. Landlords who chose to abandon Ireland left behind their castles and estates without defense. This was an invitation to the Irish to encroach on their properties. Suddenly, the resurgent Gaelic leaders were a force to reckon with. The justice office in Dublin couldn't even guarantee the safety of areas nearby. There were not enough men to mount the defenses, and in the Wicklow Mountains, the doorstep of Dublin, the O'Bryne and O'Toole chieftains waged guerrilla wars. Irish leaders accepted the English king's rule—providing he remained far away from Ireland, leaving them alone to enjoy their old traditions and follow the ancient Irish system of laws. They always challenged the authority of the royal administration and refused to recognize English law. The Irish lords declined to join the Irish Parliament, and, in time, they lost their right to vote or stand for office. Englishmen often viewed them as savages, aliens, and outlaws.

The war wasn't the only reason for the abandonment of Ireland. The north European famine struck Ireland in 1315 and lingered for many years, driving the people away to find their luck elsewhere. Another tragedy of the 14th century hit Ireland approximately at the same time—the Black Death. Dublin and Drogheda were depopulated in a matter of weeks, and the Anglo-Irish colony was panicking. There, the villages and towns were more numerous and densely populated. The bubonic plague spread through their territories like wildfire. Rural Gaelic areas were also hit, but to a much lesser extent since the population there was thin. Plague, famine, and pestilence brought a completely new level of hardship to Ireland, which was already torn up by constant feuds and battles. Many English settlers returned to the mainland, and the Gaelic resurgence continued undisturbed.

By the mid-14th century, the crisis took sway of the English colonies in Ireland. The extinction of English settlers was imminent. They begged the Crown for help, and the response came in two different ways: the dispatch of expeditions and the promulgation of laws. The Hundred Years' War was paused in 1360 with the treaty of Brétigny, allowing the Crown to dispatch resources to Ireland. King Edward III sent his son, Prince Lionel, as head of an expedition of 1,500 men. They arrived in Ireland in September of 1361 and mounted a defense against the Gaelic. The prince stayed in Ireland for five years and acted as the head of the government. He summoned Parliament in 1366 and issued the Statutes of Kilkenny, the ordinances which codified colonial legislation forbidding the English to adapt to Irish culture, and more. The most important of these ordinances forbade the Irish brehon law, private wars, and the selling of weapons to the Gaelic during wartime and food and horses during peace. The formal division between the Anglo-Irish and Gaelic church societies was also formally recognized. Prince Lionel tried to bring order to Ireland with these ordinances, but they proved unenforceable in most cases. Even his military campaigns against the Irish ultimately failed to bring royal control over the territories he owned, let alone other English lords across the island. As soon as he departed, complaints that English rule was in ruins started again.

William of Windsor led another expedition in 1369. He was an experienced veteran who had served the Crown in the wars against France. He stayed in Ireland until 1372, but he came back once more in 1373 and stayed until 1376. He is remembered for implementing heavy taxes on the Anglo-Irish, which he used to finance his army. Although he was tasked with reconquering the island, William personally never had such grand ambitions. He preferred to wage small wars, which were more often of s defensive nature. He did create and maintain local garrisons across Ireland but only so he could mount efficient defenses when needed. In the late 14th century, the local Anglo-Irish lords realized they would have to raise their armies to defend themselves successfully, as William Windsor failed to protect the royal town of Limerick, which was burned by O'Toole's forces. They stopped sending money to the Crown so they could pay for the soldiers, and the Crown needed to find a new source of money. The king tried to compel the absentee landholders to return to Ireland by issuing a statute that threatened their possessions in Ireland would be forfeited to the Crown. Nevertheless, this statute failed. The absentee lords preferred to sell their Irish possessions than to return and pay to defend them. Most of the abandoned land was already settled by the Irish, who had taken advantage of the absence of the landholders.

By 1375, Art MacMurrough Kavanagh (1357–1417) proclaimed himself King of Leinster, and the O'Briens took Munster. In Connacht, only the Anglo-Irish family of Burks represented a thin layer of English among the predominantly Irish society. In eastern Ulster, only a few thriving Anglo-Irish settlements remained. If the English wanted to take back control of Ireland, they would have to take radical measures. However, Edward III was not willing, and the matter would have to wait for the coming of age of his grandson Richard II (r. 1377–99), as he was only ten years old when he became king. But once Richard turned his attention towards Ireland, he did so in a very spectacular way. He was the first king to come to Ireland in 1210, and he came with a force numbering around 10,000 men. Richard gained the opportunity to impose his authority over Ireland by creating a truce in the Hundred Years' War and the war with Scotland. His wars in Ireland were successful. He drove MacMurrough to destruction and forced him to agree to a treaty. The Irish King of Leinster formally submitted on January 5, 1395. One of Richard's demands was for Art MacMurrough to leave Leinster, which the Irish leader obeyed. It took only a few months for Richard II to gain the submission of the great Gaelic lords: O'Bryne, O'Toole, O'Nolan, and O'Neill. They waged war between January and April 1395, and by that time, the lords had all submitted. Richard was ready to leave the island on May 15, confident he had left Ireland in peace and order.

But war soon broke out again, and Richard was forced to return to Ireland in 1399 since his heir-presumptive, Mortimer (1374–98), had been killed in battle. Richard came with a small army, but he couldn't do much before he had to set sail again. In England, Henry Bolingbroke had usurped the throne and ruled as Henry IV (r. 1399–1413). For the rest of the Middle Ages, English rulers didn't come back to Ireland, although they did pass the title "Lord of Ireland" to their heirs. England was preoccupied with dynastic troubles and foreign (Hundred Years' War) and domestic (War of the Roses) wars, which left the monarchy so weak it couldn't pay attention to Irish concerns. The English colony on the island was left to its own devices. Throughout the 15th century, it constantly had to defend itself because the Irish lords had renounced their fealty to the English king soon after Richard's departure. The Anglo-Irish and English started losing territories again and were slowly assimilated into Gaelic society. By the middle of the 1400s, the Gaelic lords held more than 65 percent of Ireland. To protect what little land they still possessed, the Anglo-Irish opted to pay the "black rent," a bribe to Gaelic lords to refrain from attacking. English residents started leaving the island again, and the landowners heavily depended on Irish tenants. The English governmental rule was limited to Pale-Dublin and the surrounding areas, approximately twenty miles (32km) from the town.

Ireland in the 15th Century

The Gaelic Ireland was divided into a patchwork of territories ruled by local lords. The power brokers were the three earldoms: Ormond, Desmond, and Kildare. In North Munster, the Desmond clan acquired power through marriage with the MacCarthy chiefs. In fact, they amassed so much power that even the Anglo-Irish towns became subjected to their authority. James Butler, the fourth Earl of Ormond, annexed the royal town of Kilkenny, including the lands belonging to the church. He founded his own local assembly, which acted as the equivalent of the Irish Parliament, exercising the powers of legislation and tax collection. In Meath, the earls of Kildare held lordship over Irish chiefs, and in the mid-15th century, they started extending their influence northwards. There, the O'Neill chiefs of Tyrone lent the lords their military help. Royal authority was completely absent, and both the Butlers and Desmonds sought to become main protectors of English interests in Ireland. Their rivalry was so intense that their efforts to repel their Gaelic neighbors fell into the second plan. The Anglo-Irish families often made alliances with the Gaelic war chiefs so they could more effectively fight their dynastic battles. But the Gaelic leaders had their own family feuds, squabbling among different branches of the same clan, and they attempted to seize the territory of their enemies, using the newly created alliances. These alliances between the Anglo-Irish and the Gaelic were unstable and often broke up. Such frequent power shifts meant that each family, whether it was Anglo-Irish or Irish, could extend its control no further than its ability to enforce it. The Anglo-Irish earldoms of Desmond and Ormond remained too powerful for any revival of native rule, and no Irish lord had enough power to challenge the Anglo-Irish landlords.

None of the Irish families managed to revive the high kingship, and the best they could hope for was a confederation, which would help them battle the Anglo-Irish challenge. In the 15th century, several attempts were made to create such a confederation, but they all failed. The native lords were unable to create long-lasting alliances, but even if they succeeded, there was no guarantee they would be powerful enough to battle the Anglo-Irish landlords. These landholders were scattered around, but they held the territories that were most densely populated and yielded the most from agriculture. Agriculture had been the main moneymaker of the previous centuries, but significant changes occurred during the 15th century. Norman settlers concentrated on tilling the land and created a surplus of grain crops for export. But a new trend came in the late Middle Ages: pastoral farming. Suddenly, this concentration shifted from agriculture to cattle and sheep products. The domestic cloth industry developed, and the export of sheep wool declined while demand for cattle hides rose. Other export materials included timber, as Ireland still had extensive forests, and wild animal hides such as fox, squirrel, and otter. Fish was always a staple export of Ireland, but towards the end of the 15th century, this shifted to the linen and cloth industry. Much of the Irish linen and cloth products were exported, and the most famous was the Irish mantle, a distinguished article. Fishing still brought steady income, but mainly because the Spanish and English fishing fleets paid local communities money for the rights to exploit nearby waters. Ireland even started importing herring from Spain, as well as iron for tool production, salt for food conservation, and wine. Most trades were in the hands of Anglo-Irish and English merchants who acquired proper licenses, although some native Irish consumers and producers became essential participants in urban markets.

The Anglo-Irish continued to demand a high level of autonomy, but they never seriously thought of completely breaking off from the English Crown. They made sure to put their own people in the government of Ireland, and soon they started privatizing and monopolizing the administration in Dublin. In the 15th century, the position of justiciar was referred to as lord-lieutenant—chief governor of the colony. From the 1420s until the 1440s, the frequent holder of that office was the Earl of Ormond, and he staked the House of Commons with his people, even those who supported the Irish. They often invited English and Irish to take up arms in support of the earl's agenda whenever a political opponent held the governor's post. The main enemy of the Earl of Ormond was Sir John Talbot, the first Earl of Shrewsbury who was in a political alliance with his brother Richard Talbot, Archbishop of Dublin. This rivalry between the Butlers and Talbots split the Anglo-Irish colony for generations. In reality, this split was only mirroring one of the English Wars of the Roses, a civil war that involved the rival aristocratic houses of Lancaster (red rose) and York (white rose), who competed for the English throne. John Butler and his Ormond forces sided with the Lancasters, and just like their role models in England, they too were defeated at the Battle of Piltown in 1462. Thomas Fitzgerald was the victor, and he became the most powerful man in Ireland. In 1463, Fitzgerald became the eighth Earl of Desmond and lord-lieutenant of Ireland, proclaimed so by the newly installed York king, Edward IV (r. 1461–70 and 1471–83).

The Earl of Desmond was very popular, and like his predecessors, he started making alliances with the Gaelic lords. This resulted in his rise to tremendous power. However, this was exactly what King Edward had forbidden him to do. His actions brought the wrath of the English residents of Pale, who accused him of extorting coins from them to support his private army. Edward IV finally actively intervened by appointing Sir John Tiptoft (ca. 1427–70), earl of Worcester, as chief governor. Sir Tiptoft was known as "the Butcher of England" because he ruthlessly executed anyone who dared to stand against the king. He accused Earl of Desmond and his brother-in-law, the Earl of Kildare, of treason because they were allies with the native Irish. He summoned them both to answer for their crimes and had them both beheaded on February 14, 1468. Both the Anglo-Irish and Gaelic were appalled by this, and they rose in rebellion, forcing the king to recall Sir John Tiptoft. By 1487, they also convinced the king to put the Earl of Kildare in the governmental office. The Kildare representative, known as "Garret Mor" (Big Garret) Fitzgerald, set out to secure absolute control over the government. He wasn't the most powerful among the Anglo-Irish lords, but he had one great advantage: his earldom's geographical position. Kildare's proximity to Dublin gave Garret an amazing strategic position to quickly and firmly seize power. As lord-lieutenant of Ireland, he had absolute control over Parliament and its members. He used his political power and influence— not to make himself an independent ruler but to promote the York cause. He remained loyal to the king and the English dynasty.

In 1487, the Earl of Kildare played kingmaker when he refused to acknowledge the victory and coronation of the Lancastrian claimant to the throne, Henry VII (r. 1485-1509). Instead, he welcomed Lambert Simnel (1475-1535), the nephew of Edward IV, to Ireland. Lambert was then crowned King of England and Dublin on May 24, 1487. But when Lambert returned to England, he failed to secure his title. In 1491, Fitzgerald welcomed another York claimant to the English throne, Perkin Warbeck (ca. 1474-99). This time, both the Earl of Desmond and Earl of Kildare conspired to put him on the throne, but ultimately they failed. Insecure on his throne, Henry VII saw Ireland as a refuge for his political opponents, and in 1494, he sent Sir Edward Poynings, a soldier and administrator, to summon the Irish Parliament. The result was a reaffirmation of the Statutes of Kilkenny, in which all English and Anglo-Irish settlers were prohibited from using the law and customs, but not the language. For, by now, the Irish language was widely spoken, and English was restricted to Pale and some of the larger towns. But the most celebrated provision was Poynings' Law, which forbade the Irish Parliament from assembling without the king's approval. It also required royal consent of all legislation before its passage in the Parliament of Dublin. This law was the Crown's attempt to take away the ability of the lord-lieutenant to summon Parliament and use it against the king or the royal interests.

Sir Edward Poynings suspected that the Earl of Kildare, Garret Mor, had allied himself with the Irish who resided in the north, and he ordered his arrest and imprisonment on charges of treason. As before, this act only instigated widespread rebellions in which the Irish attacked the borders of the counties Louth, Meath, Dublin, and Kildare. King Henry VII lacked the money and military to deal with Ireland, and he was unable to do anything else but to reinstall Garret, Earl of Kildare, as lord-lieutenant in 1499. He remained in this position until he died in 1513, and he was succeeded by his son, "Garret Og" (Young Garret) Fitzgerald (1487–1534).

Chapter 5 – The Protestant Power in Ireland

Depiction of Hugh O'Neill on a fresco in Vatican

In the 16th century, Europe was divided by religion. With demands for the reformation of the church made by Martin Luther in Germany, Protestantism started spreading. But the 16th century in England also saw the rise of the House of Tudor and the two longest-reigning rulers, Henry VIII and his daughter Elizabeth I, who sought to consolidate their power in all English possessions. Henry's departure from the Roman Catholic Church in 1534 brought the need to make England protestant, which would be safe from further religious turmoil that raged across Europe. Henry VIII and Elizabeth sought to reconquer Ireland and plant Protestantism there. However, the Anglo-Irish acted as the protectors of Catholicism, and English power diminished. In the English view, the Anglo-Irish were as disloyal as the Gaelic Irish. As such, they were considered rebels and culturally inferior people. Protestantism wasn't the only thing the English kings tried to plant in Ireland. They recolonized the island with English people loyal to the Crown, attempting to remove the natives and replace them with their own people, who, they hoped, would take root in Ireland.

But this planting of people in Ireland was a work in progress, and it needed time. Still, the goal of completely replacing the natives was never truly achieved. In 1598, the great Earl of Ulster, Hugh O'Neill, was defeated. He was the symbol of Irish resistance, and his fall marked the zenith of the native population. Nevertheless, the Catholic will to resist persevered. The native Irish were joined by the Anglo-Irish Catholic landowners to mount one of the largest-scale rebellions in Ireland in 1641, but their Catholic insurgence was crushed, and they lost most of their land. Their religion was ruthlessly repressed, and the armies of Oliver Cromwell's Puritans stormed the island. Only when Charles II was restored to the throne did the Catholics gain momentum, which they used to once again become the dominant religion in Ireland. Under King James II, who was Catholic himself, the Irish had a moment of peace, but in England, the dynastic power struggle led to his overthrow and the installation of Protestant William III. Once again, the fights between Catholics and Protestants ensued, and the result was the Catholic loss of the right to own land, whether they were Gaelic Irish or Anglo-Irish. All this fighting only cemented the division of Irish society. People were already divided on a racial basis, and now the religious battle added a whole new layer of division. The English were Protestants, and the Irish were Catholics, and the settlement of 1693 gave political and economic power to the English.

The Society of Ireland in 16th Century

The society of Ireland consisted of segmented people who lived side by side. The Gaelic Irish had around sixty lords of greater or lesser status. Some of them were the descendants of old provincial kings, and their authority was always completely independent of England. In Ulster, where the English presence was reduced to a few scattered settlements, the Gaelic Irish were most powerful. The Gaelic lords maintained complete control over the lands there, but their compatriots could be found all over Ireland. There were Kavanagh and O'Bryne in Leinster, O'Connor and O'Kelly in Connacht, and O'Brien and MacCarthy in Munster. The Irish population of these territories didn't recognize the authority of the English king or lords. They only responded to their Gaelic leaders, and the English viewed them as enemies of the Crown. Gaelic Irish lords shared rule over the land with the great Anglo-Irish lords. The contemporary English observed the Anglo-Irish as the rebel English. They were too adapted to Gaelic culture and even spoke the language. The Anglo-Irish were led by the powerful family of Fitzgerald of Kildare. During the early reign of Henry VIII, the eighth and ninth Earl of Kildare served as lord-lieutenant of Ireland. Other Anglo-Irish lords included the Desmond Fitzgeralds, Barrys, Powers in Munster; Butlers, Dillons, and Tyrrells in Leinster; the Burkes in Connacht; and several completely isolated families. They all recognized the authority of the English Crown but largely operated independently.

The Crown had complete control only over the English Pale and the territories of river valleys in the east and southeast of Ireland. These areas were inhabited by the "Old English" residents, the descendants of Norman conquerors. They were government officials, merchants, lower gentry, and professionals. In the eyes of English society, they were the only ones of high economic and civil positions to be regarded as cosmopolitan. They were eager to expand their jurisdiction and trade in other Irish territories, and they stubbornly opposed both the Gaelic and the Anglo-Irish.

Irish and English regions were very different in economic aspects. Rural life prevailed everywhere, and semi-nomadic pastoral farming was the main lifestyle of the population. It proved very useful to be able to quickly move the household and its livestock in a country where wars were common. The countryside was filled with enormous herds of cattle and sheep whose value was in their milk, skin, and wool, not their meat. Isolated farms existed, but they were scattered all over the landscape of Ireland. One family-clan would rent the land, and they could number anywhere between a dozen and several hundred. This communal system was called *rundale*, and every household would have a small unfenced share of land for tilling and nearby pastureland. This land would be redistributed among the family members upon the death of the head of the household. Some clans implemented a new law of redistributing the land on an annual basis. This ensured that all the members of the community had enough land to sustain them.

The Anglo-Irish settlements contrasted with those of the Gaelic. The Anglo-Irish had more advanced agricultural practices, and tenants possessed the most fertile land of Ireland. They were familiar with the agronomy of southern England, which allowed them to cultivate a wide range of crops. In Gaelic territories, the spade remained the main tilling tool, but the Anglo-Irish already used the plow. The population lived in villages or permanent communities, so they did not need to move. Anglo-Irish settlements had shops, markets, and churches, all located very near the large manor houses in which the lords and their family resided. But commercial life was restricted to towns, which were largely populated by the English. The Gaelic chieftains demanded heavy taxes for the right to trade on their territory, which made the existence of the towns there impossible. English merchants concentrated mostly in the port towns from which they could handle overseas trade. But this trade was very limited, usually to domestic hides, tallow, and linen. They would import salt, wine, and manufactured goods.

The 16th century was also known for very limited church authority. The greedy chieftains and lords usurped the religious hierarchy, and secular powers replaced it. Since Ireland was so cut off from Rome and had little to no papal influence, the priesthood became a hereditary profession in Gaelic areas. The Irish leaders made provisions to support the clerics, just like they did with the lawyers and the bards. They considered these professionals to be their clients. But the appointment of episcopal titles was largely reserved for the kinsmen of lords and chieftains. Even in the English territories of Ireland, the lords strived to appoint the bishops, most often from among the members of their own noble houses. The monks of the Franciscan order, who mostly operated in Gaelic territories, were the first to demand religious reforms. They called for spiritual renewal and the end of the lords' control over the church. Once Henry VIII started radical changes to impose royal authority over the church, the Irish monks were the first to oppose him.

Henry VIII, King of Ireland

During the first half of his rule, Henry VIII (1491-1547) was preoccupied with the wars in Europe, and he paid little attention to Ireland. His main concern throughout his reign was to consolidate his power. In the 1530s, it became evident that he had no authority whatsoever in Ireland. The Earls of Kildare monopolized the power, which attracted the attention of the English monarch. Henry felt that his monarchy was threatened and that he needed to take action in Ireland. But he preferred a peaceful solution because his resources were already stretched thin by the commitments and wars he waged elsewhere. In the end, the king mixed martial means with diplomacy to secure his authority on the island.

Henry was determined to curb the independent-acting Anglo-Irish and leading Irish families. That mainly meant dealing with the Fitzgeralds of Kildare. At that moment, Lord-lieutenant Gerald FitzGerald, "Garret Og," was working tirelessly to convert this governmental office into a hereditary title. He left for England in 1534, but first, he made sure that his son Thomas, Lord Offaly ("Silken Thomas," 1513–37), was made lord-lieutenant. Just like his father, Thomas wasted no time and immediately challenged royal authority. In June 1534, he launched a rebellion that lasted for one year and two months. In the end, the rebellion was quelled by Sir William Skeffington, the representative of the king. Silken Thomas surrendered in August 1535, and the king had him executed, together with his five uncles. The rebellion was the start of the downfall of the House of Kildare. But it was also the beginning of Anglo-Irish predominance in Ireland. From the day the rebellion ended, all appointed lord-lieutenants were Englishmen.

On June 18, 1541, the Irish Parliament held a session in which it was decided that Henry VIII and his successors would no longer bear the title "Lord of Ireland." but "King of Ireland." This parliament had many Anglo-Irish and Gaelic Irish in attendance, and they all had to swear an oath to the English king. Henry took the crown of Ireland because he needed to see the island secured under English rule. He led a campaign to try to persuade the Anglo-Irish and Irish to accept the fact that the English Crown had authority over their island. The next lord-lieutenant, Anthony St. Leger, passed a policy of "Surrender and Regrant." This meant that if landlords were to surrender their possessions and give them to the

Crown, the Crown would give them back as feudal fiefs. Those who agreed to this were made nobles. The O'Briens became earls of Thomond. But in return for the fiefs, the Irish were expected to obey English laws and customs. The Irish who acknowledged this policy were given the same status as the Anglo-Irish. They now had access to royal courts and the full protection guaranteed by English law. "Surrender and Regrant" proved to be attractive, as even the great lord of Ulster, Evan O'Neill, traveled to London to kneel before the king and swear an oath of loyalty. In return, he was made Earl of Tyrone. By the end of Henry VIII's reign, more than forty Irish lords had submitted to the English Crown.

But Henry's campaign wasn't enough, as not all Irish were so easily persuaded. In most cases, the policy of "Surrender and Regrant" was only nominally followed, and back on their soil, the Irish would continue to act as before, disregarding the English laws. Militant royal officials soon arrived to confiscate and reconquest the island, undermining the diplomacy work. Eager English land seekers seized territories in the middle of Leinster and convinced the Irish lords that the ultimate goal of the Crown was to take away their properties. But Henry was stubborn and insisted on making the Irish his loyal subjects. However, with the introduction of the religious reforms, he only managed to push them further away from the idea of recognizing his authority.

In 1534, Henry abolished the pope's jurisdiction in England because Rome denied him the right to divorce his wife, Queen Cathrine of Aragon, who failed to give him a son. Henry wanted to make sure his dynasty continued to occupy the English throne, but without a son, this dream was in jeopardy. He proclaimed himself the "Supreme Head of the Church of England" to be able to divorce and remarry. By 1536, he cut off all the English church's ties with the Roman Catholic Church. As he was the ruler of England and Ireland, he wanted to impose the same religious doctrines in all his realms. The Irish Parliament passed the act that acknowledged King Henry VIII as the sole head of the Church of Ireland, and the royal government started closing monasteries across the land, which had already been done in England. By closing the monasteries, the royal family gained incredible wealth.

But in Ireland, the conversion and confiscation of the church land wasn't as simple as in England. The native monks were crying for the restoration of the church's powers, not its complete dissolution. These monks were quick to gain the support of Gaelic and Anglo-Irish lords. They depicted the Fitzgeralds of Kildare as crusaders against religious reform, and they gladly accepted the role. The native Irish had separately organized churches, and the religious changes that the king wanted to implement gave them a reason to push for Irish independence. The Crown anticipated Gaelic Irish and Anglo-Irish opposition to the change, but it was completely taken by surprise when the "Old English" joined in the resistance, too. They had always been loyal to the Crown, and their involvement in the rebellion would carry consequences that would shape the history of Ireland. In the territories where the English resided, many clergymen were unwilling to accept the religious reformation. They preferred to resign their posts. Many lawyers, merchants, and even government officials withdrew their sons from the English universities, which were now staffed by Protestant teachers. They sent them to European universities, where the Jesuits, an order created specifically as counter-reformation in 1540, were teaching.

After the death of Henry VIII, religious reforms continued under the rule of his successors, Edward IV (r. 1547–53) and Elizabeth I (r. 1558-1603). The only exception was Queen Mary I (r. 1553–58), as she was a devout Catholic who restored the old faith in England. The Church of Ireland was sanctioned, but it continued to operate, copying the Roman Catholic prelate. The head of the church was the Archbishop of Armagh, and he was responsible for the Church of Ireland island-wide. At the same time, he served as the bishop of Armagh. He enjoyed all the privileges once reserved for the Catholic high clergymen. Nobody ever knew the precise religious convictions of Queen Elizabeth, and they remain a mystery, as she centered her rule around politics, not religion. For her, maintaining royal supremacy was the main concern, and the questions of religion only served this purpose. When she began her rule, Elizabeth was an inexperienced young woman, the daughter of Henry VIII and his second wife, Anne Boleyn. Because her father had annulled that marriage, Elizabeth was considered his illegitimate child; therefore, her grasp on the throne of England was very insecure. Elizabeth never had a burning zeal for Protestant principles, and she was tolerant of her Catholic subjects. But she could not abide the disloyal ones. The Catholics were the ones who considered her illegitimate, and because of this, she needed to proceed with the alignment of her realms with the religious group that accepted her as their queen.

By the Elizabethan Settlement of 1559, the English monarch was declared to be the only supreme governor of both ecclesiastical and temporal matters. Central doctrines of Protestant worship were laid down in the Second Book of Common Prayer (1552) and later again in the Thirty-nine Articles of 1563. This only hardened the religious division in England and Ireland. Irish Parliament passed the Act of Elizabethan Settlement in 1560, making the queen head of the state and Church of Ireland. All governmental officials, tenants-in-chief, university professors, town mayors, and newly-appointed earls and nobles were forced to accept and acknowledge the queen's new status. The same year, the Irish Parliament passed the Act of Uniformity, issued in England a year earlier, by which all clergy were required to use the Book of Common Prayer as the only sacred doctrine. The English language was decreed as the language of the Book, and in Ireland, the church had to pay a fine if it used Gaelic.

Queen Elizabeth's reforms encountered much harder resistance in Ireland than those of her father, mainly because Henry kept Orthodox Catholic doctrines intact. She was excommunicated by Pope Pius V (r. 1566–72), which meant that her Catholic subjects were absolved from being obedient to her. The Gaelic Irish had long ago resented the foreign government of their lands, and these religious reforms only added to that resentment. Even the Old English remained loyal to Catholicism in Ireland, which meant they were no longer loyal to the Crown. They refused to participate in state religion and thus were ineligible to occupy state offices. The English government used the newly escalated situation in Ireland to appoint Protestant-born Englishman to the offices in Dublin. By getting rid of the disobedient English and Anglo-Irish from the Irish Parliament, the English Crown was able to take more direct control over the island.

Elizabeth's Control Over Ireland

Under Queen Elizabeth, England started developing its nationalism, made up of economic dominance in the known world, militant Protestantism, and cultural arrogance. All of this was reflected in Ireland, where aggression towards English policies was growing. In England, calls were made for the permanent disposal of Catholic landowners, but at first, Elizabeth wasn't motivated. She wanted to advance the English interests in Ireland, but not if it would cost her the government. So, she decided to tread carefully. Lord-lieutenant Thomas Radclyffe (r.1560-1564) called for a military settlement of the midland territories and restoration of the English practices in Anglo-Irish lordships. He started building up the army, but the English residents of Pale, afraid of newly-imposed taxes which were to supply the militia, managed to convince the government to dispose of him. The next lord-lieutenant, Sir Henry Sidney of Sussex (r. 1565-1571), set about defeating the stubborn lord of Ulster, Shane O'Neill (ca 1530–1570), who refused to hold the title of an English vassal. Shane O'Neill preferred to remain

Irish chieftain and to follow the old Irish laws. Shane eluded the lord-lieutenant, but ultimately he was murdered by the rival house of O'Donnells. He was succeeded by his second cousin, Turlough Luineach O'Neill (ca. 1530–95).

In the meantime, James Fitzmaurice Fitzgerald (d. 1579) led a rebellion in Munster that lasted for five years. It was suppressed in 1573 when James was banished to the continent. In the same year, Walter Devereux, First Earl of Essex, started an expedition to Ulster to subdue its Irish lord. But the guerilla-style skirmishes of the local lords managed to prevent Lord Essex from achieving much. He switched his tactics from small-scale attacks to large-scale raids and massacres. The most famous massacre occurred in 1575 when he ordered his naval forces to land on Rathlin Island. Hundreds of women and children of the MacDonell clan were murdered. Ultimately, the Essex expedition failed. Sir Henry Sidney of Sussex was recalled to serve in Ireland, and his second term as lord-lieutenant lasted from 1575 until 1578. Fitzmaurice Fitzgerald returned to Ireland in 1579, leading a small army, intending to launch a second rebellion against English authority over the island. He gained the support of Munster's Anglo-Irish and Gaelic lords and the Gaelic residents of Pale. But, by 1583, the government managed to quell this rebellion and kill all the ringleaders, including the Earl of Desmond. His lands were confiscated by the Crown. This mighty earldom was crushed, and the government made sure it instigated no more rebellions. The territory of Munster was now settled by loyal English subjects. Approximately 4,000 English residents were installed in the territory once held by the Earl of Desmond. The government made sure that the new settlers were not only English but also Protestants. Control of Ireland was in the hands of the English Crown, and during the 1580s and 1590s, its claim was unchallenged.

The Nine Years' War (1593-1603)

Queen Elizabeth managed to secure her authority in Ireland by the 1590s, with only one exception. In the heartland of Ulster province, the government and culture remained entirely Gaelic. The two strongest Ulster families ruled the entire region: the O'Neills in Tyrone (Tír Eóghain) and the O'Donnells in Tyrconnell (Tír Conaill) and its close surrounding areas. These two families were allies against the English but rivals between themselves. In the eyes of the Crown, they were both stubborn, rebellious chieftains who threatened English integrity. The Ulsters, on the other hand, looked with resentment on English land seekers and the English laws the Crown was trying to impose on them. They wanted to preserve their native culture and Gaelic power in the region.

Hugh O'Neill (Aodh Mór Ó Neill, 1540-1616), Second Earl of Tyrone, was the grandson of Conn O'Neill, who had surrendered to the Crown back in 1542. Hugh's father lost the title once his brother, Shane O'Neill, challenged him. Young Hugh spent his childhood in England, under the protection of the queen. There he learned modern methods of warfare and dreamed about avenging his father. Once he returned to Ireland, he brought a band of English adventurers, who helped him secure the southern part of Tyrone under his control. The English supported his elevation to the title of Second Earl of Tyrone, as they hoped he would be their accomplice in Ulster. But Hugh was calculating and smart. He concluded that ultimately, the English were a bigger threat to his ambitions than his own family, the O'Neills. In 1593, his cousin, Turlough Luineach O'Neill, abdicated the lordship, and Hugh took over. However, the English Crown refused to acknowledge him as the First Earl of Tyrone. To challenge the English rule in Ireland, in 1595, he assumed the Gaelic title of chieftain. Hugh's actions resulted in English opposition. First to voice their dissatisfaction were the minor government officials, and in the end, the lord-lieutenant joined them. But Hugh raised a defense against possible English retaliation, and he became known among his people as the "Great Earl." He also allied with Red Hugh O'Donnell (Aodh Rua Ó Domhnaill, 1541-1602), prince of Tyrconnell. He also sought support from the other Gaelic citizens of Ireland. He needed this island-wide support because he realized that only by expelling the English from Ireland would his title and position be secured.

At the beginning of the rebellion, Ulster was the offensive force. There, Hugh organized musket men, cavalry, and infantry using pikes, imitating the tactics he knew the English army used. But he also employed Bonnaghts, native Irish mercenaries, and gallowglasses from Scotland. These two mercenary groups fought in the traditional Irish manner—harassing and ambushing the enemy. In 1597, the English had enough of this harassment and decided to march directly into the Irish areas, leaving the safety of their garrisons and fortresses. This decision made by inept English commanders proved to be fatal, as O'Neill defeated them at Yellow Ford, just north of Armagh. The battle was fought on August 14, 1598, and it served as an awakening call for the English, who finally realized that the Irish were a formidable opponent. Queen Elizabeth was alarmed, and she sent Sir Robert Devereux (1566-1601), the Second Earl of Essex, to assume the position of lord-lieutenant and lead her forces. He arrived in Ireland with an army of 17,000 men, but he met defeat on every occasion. By September, the queen ordered him back to England. The next lord-lieutenant was Baron Mountjoy, Charles Blount (ca. 1562-1606). He arrived in Ireland in 1600 and personally led a campaign that saw the establishment of many new garrisons. But he also led scorched-earth tactics—burning crops, houses, and livestock so the Irish would starve. At Derry, he used naval forces to land behind O'Neill and coordinated a double attack.

O'Neill knew he needed the support of all of Ireland, so he went on a campaign in which he presented himself as the champion of Counter-Reformation. This call failed to impress the Anglo-Irish, but he did succeed in getting the attention of the Spanish King Philip IV (r. 1598-1616). Spain was already an enemy of England in the 16th century and was eager to help the Irish cause. Philip IV sent an army of 4,400 Spanish soldiers, which landed at Kinsale in September 1601. But the foreign meddling in domestic matters only added new urgency to the rebellion. England feared that the Spaniards would use Ireland as a backdoor to launch a full-scale attack on the heart of the kingdom. When the Spanish arrived, the Irish forces hurried south to meet them. But Mountjoy also led the English southwards, intending to occupy the Spanish army before the Irish could come to their help. On Christmas Eve 1601, O'Neill and O'Donnell's forces laid siege on Mountjoy's forces, who were themselves besieging the Spanish. But the Irish were not well organized, and their cavalry deserted them, allowing Mountjoy to overrun his enemy. The English completely defeated both Irish and Spanish forces, forcing the latter to sail home. O'Donnell joined the fleet and escaped to Spain, panicking after the gruesome defeat. But he hoped to secure further assistance from Philip IV. Unfortunately, he died in Spain the next year.

Defeated, O'Neill led his forces back to Ulster. There he was joined by Red Hugh O'Donnell's younger brother, Rory (Rudhraighe Ó Domhnaill, 1575-1608). They continued to lead the rebellion but suffered defeat after defeat and were unable to break the streak of bad luck. Because of Mountjoy's ruthless scorched-earth tactics, the rebels were unable to live in the countryside. The Irish population was starving, and the rebel leaders couldn't do anything to relieve them. In March of 1603, O'Neill opened negotiations with the Crown's representative, admitting defeat. The Nine Years' War, otherwise known as Tyrone's Rebellion, was the largest-scale resistance to English rule in Ireland during the 16th century. Even though it ultimately failed, this rebellion opened the eyes of the English, who worked even harder to secure their grasp over Ireland.

The war transformed the whole scene of Ireland, particularly Ulster province. English authority was everywhere, and no part of the island was out of its reach. However, the O'Neills and O'Donnells remained favorites of the Gaelic Irish, and they managed to maintain their prestige. The English government preferred not to anger the Irish and decided not to punish the two families responsible for the rebellion. The treaty was signed on March 30, 1603, and it specified that the O'Neills were permitted to keep their titles and lands. The O'Donnells, on the other hand, were elevated, and their leader, Rory O'Donnell, became the First Earl of Tyrconnell. But these were English titles, and they meant little to nothing to the prestige they enjoyed as the princes of Ireland. Both the O'Neills and the O'Donnells spent the next several years resenting the fact that they had become English subjects, mere landowners in service to the Crown.

Hugh O'Neill was called to London because of some minor land dispute. However, he knew this was just an excuse to execute him because his family was a thorn in the English heel since his son had served in the Spanish army. On the night of September 14, 1607, O'Neill and Rory O'Donnell set sail for Spain, choosing voluntary exile to the continent. Their escape is remembered in the history of Ireland as the "The Flight of the Earls." They were followed by their wider family, numbering ninety-nine nobles altogether. Spain refused to receive them, so they continued their voyage to Rome, where Pope Paul V welcomed them as champions of the Roman Catholic Church. O'Neill and O'Donnell had the intention of securing foreign help and returning to Ireland. They spent nine years in self-exile, searching for willing allies, but with no success. Hugh O'Neill died in 1616 in Rome. The "Flight of the Earls" left Ulster without a leader, and the power vacuum created was an opportunity for the English to reshape society. King James I (r. 1603-1625) was eager to plant Protestants in the territory of Ulster and remove the thorn of the Gaelic Irish once and for all.

During the reign of King James I, the first Stuart king of England, plans were drawn to confiscate all the land of six counties in Ulster: Tyrone, Fermanagh, Donegal, Coleraine, Cavan, and Armagh. The land was to be sold to Scottish and English Protestants under favorable terms. Those who could not afford to buy the land would be renting it directly from the Crown. Similar plans were made for the foundation of new, purely Protestant towns in the region. In such a manner, the city of Belfast came to be. Founded by the charter of April 27, 1613, its Irish name, *Beal Feirste*, means "mouth of the Feirste River," symbolizing the location of the city. Thousands of people arrived in Ireland during the early 16th century. Some came from England, but the majority came from Scotland. They were all Protestants, and they brought with them their institutions and culture. In a very short period, the way of life in Ulster changed completely.

But the Irish Catholics were not completely displaced. Many newcomers found it much easier to employ the native Irish to work as the agricultural labor force, so the population ended up being religiously mixed. However, those Catholics who were fortunate enough to remain tenants were forced to occupy the least productive land. The Catholics were resentful, but they waited for the right opportunity for revenge. The new population in Ulster was "New English," their religion separating them from the "Old English" who were still Catholics but loyal to the Crown. Nevertheless, the latter was still seen as a population that harbored treasonous sentiments.

Éirí Amach - The Rebellion of 1641

Thomas Wentworth (1593-1641) became the administrator of Ireland in 1633. He was cunning, ambitious, and ruthless. He built an efficient, independent administration of Ireland with the purpose of gaining wealth for his king, Charles I (r. 1625-49), who had succeeded James I. However, Thomas also gathered considerable wealth for himself through various land investments. He first secured the election of men loyal to him into the Irish Parliament. He also instigated many quarrels between the Catholics and Protestants, earning the distrust of both factions. His government completely disregarded local interests and continued confiscating Catholic land in Connacht. The English Catholics were particularly angry because the government made no distinction between them and the Irish Catholics; both suffered land confiscation equally. Protestants were not treated much better, as Wentworth decided to penalize the Ulster plantation settlers for employing the native Irish instead of Protestants. Also, the Presbyterian Scots were restricted from practicing their religion. None of these factions was ready to challenge Wentworth while he was in Ireland, but when he was recalled to England in 1639, they came together to destroy the government he left behind. The Irish Parliament convinced the English one to secure a charge of treason against Thomas Wentworth, and he was executed in 1641.

King Charles I faced open war with Presbyterians in Scotland, and he couldn't afford to antagonize the Irish. He granted the "Graces" to the Catholics, a concession that included the abolition of fines for the practice of Roman Catholicism and the end of religious tests for inheritance tax (Catholics paid higher inheritance tax than Protestants). But after the dispatch of Thomas Wentworth, the religious factions of Ireland were in a state of confusion. The Catholics feared the Protestant militarism that was on the rise in the Irish Parliament. On the other hand, the "New English" Protestants felt insecurity in their newly-acquired properties. They didn't know if they should support Parliament or the king who sought to rule without Parliament restraining his authority. The native Irish once again felt the need to demand more rights, and they openly expressed their rebellious sentiment.

The English Catholics went further and started demanding even more rights from the king. They wanted wider independent powers for the Irish Parliament because they believed that only self-governance would ensure them the rights to own property and freedom of religion. But the king wouldn't allow further diminishing of his authority. And even though the Old English wanted similar independence as the English Parliament already had, they couldn't rely on it from the king. They saw the English Parliament as a greater enemy because, while Charles I allowed Catholics' existence, Parliament was militantly Protestant and would see all Catholics expelled from the land. The king needed to keep good relations with foreign Catholic kings, so he wouldn't dare to antagonize them by completely abolishing the Roman Catholic Church. Because of this, in the early 17th century, the Catholic Church in Ireland thrived, even though it was dominated by secular chieftains. Rome made sure that the church in Ireland was taken care of, and an unofficial diocesan structure was set up. Irish prelates exiled in Catholic Europe trained the priests, which would go back to Ireland to serve. In the 17th century, they were joined by the Old English, who feared the persecution of their religion. They found common ground with the native Irish of Ulster not only in religion but also in confiscated land. In 1641, the native Irish from Ulster made a plot to capture Dublin Castle and the government's chief officials residing in it. Then, they would hold a series of uprisings demanding Catholic rights.

The plot was launched on October 23, 1641, but the Irish failed to secure Dublin Castle. Nevertheless, they managed to gain control of most of the Ulster territory. They declared themselves defenders of the king against the English Parliament, hoping to avoid the label of rebels. The organized insurrections, destroying much of the Protestant possessions in Ulster. As many as 2,000 Protestants were killed, while tens of thousands were banished to other Protestant areas in Ireland. The Ulstermen then moved south, gathering support on their way to Drogheda. There, they joined with the Old English of the area, transforming the local Uster uprising into a nationwide movement. They called themselves the "Catholic Army," and under this name, they defeated the government's army at the Battle of Julianstown on November 29, 1641. In January of the following year, they reached Limerick. The New English and the Scot settlers called for the government's reaction against the general massacre of the Protestants, but the king and the English Parliament were unable to interfere, as they were busy quarreling and starting the English Civil War of 1642. Parliament accused the king of collaborating with the Irish Catholics and withheld the money that was supposed to finance the army. Finally, in April of 1642, the English Parliament decided to send a Scottish expedition under the command of General Robert Munro (ca.1601–1680).

Old English and Gaelic Irish founded an official body known as the Kilkenny Assembly in 1642. This assembly mirrored the already-existing Irish Parliament, with an upper house comprising bishops, abbots, Catholic gentry; and a lower house comprising county and clan representatives. This assembly was an alliance of English and Irish Catholics that displayed the first signs of Irish nationalism, although in the form of a religious sect. Although it took them six weeks to make a decision, the Kilkenny Assembly sided with the rebels. Overall in Ireland, the Catholics held two-thirds of arable land, and they didn't want to lose that land—and, with it, their political influence. With cautious machinations, the Irish Catholics, now calling themselves the Confederation of Kilkenny, managed to join the efforts of the English royalists against the English Parliament. Their principles were not to sue for an independent Ireland but a Catholic Ireland that would be loyal to the Stuart king and his successors.

The nephew of Hugh O'Neill, Colonel Owen Roe O'Neill (1590-1649), arrived in Ireland after the years he spent serving the Spanish army. He was an experienced military leader, and he was aware that religiously-inspired Catholics had no other choice but to completely expel the Protestant English from the island. But that meant driving off those not only loyal to Parliament but also to the Crown. The Confederation of Kilkenny was unwilling to part ways with the English royalists and the king who had shown them tolerance. For the next seven years, confusion reigned in Ireland. O'Neill was successful in defeating Munro's Scottish army in 1646, but the Old English failed to provide him with consistent support. Because of it, Roe O'Neill was unable to score a decisive victory. Lords of Leinster were wary of O'Neill, as they thought the young general only wanted to secure all the political power for himself. They decided not to call him for aid, and they failed to dislodge the Dublin governmental forces. The Irish Catholics wasted years in negotiations with King Charles I, who only sought to stall giving more religious freedoms. Their nightmares came true when Parliament came out victorious at the end of the English Civil War in 1649.

The Parliament in London executed the king and abolished the monarchy, installing the republican Commonwealth, which immediately turned its attention towards Ireland. Oliver Cromwell (1599-1658), the leader of the English Parliament, was a staunch anti-Catholic. He arrived in Ireland in August of 1649 as commander in chief and lord-lieutenant. Cromwell launched a three-part program with the goal to eliminate all resistance to Parliament's authority, eradicate all Catholic landowners and priests who took part in the rebellion, and convert the entire population of Ireland to Protestantism. His Protestant armies carried out military reprisals and unjustified attacks, which they called revenge for the actions of the Catholic Confederacy. With his 20,000 men and the military experience gained in the English Civil War, Oliver

Cromwell crushed all opposition in Ireland. His army performed two major massacres in Drogheda and in Wexford, in which more than 6,000 individuals lost their lives. The excuse was to set examples that would shorten the Irish campaign. Cromwell spent nine months ravaging Ireland before he returned to England, believing he had succeeded in securing the island. But the efforts had to continue until 1653, when the English Parliament managed to fully conquer Ireland. The Cromwellian Settlement was imposed on Irish Catholics in 1652, by which the practice of the Roman Catholic religion was abolished. All priests were caught and executed, and a reward was offered as a bounty on those who continued to practice the faith in secrecy. All the participants of the rebellion of 1641 were caught and executed, and all the land possessed by the Catholics was confiscated. Catholics were also banned from living in towns and cities, but they could apply for land donations in Connacht. The Catholic landowning aristocracy ceased to exist in Ireland, and the wealth and power they held were simply transferred to the Protestants. By the end of the century, the Brehon law was completely eradicated, replaced by the English law and court.

Still, the Cromwellian Settlement wasn't completely successful in its intention. The promotion of Protestantism went forward, schools were opened, and Protestant clergymen were brought from England. But problems arose almost immediately, as the teachers and the preachers didn't speak Irish and were unable to communicate with their audiences. Also, the Cromwellian church favored Puritanism and the Presbyterian sect, which the Anglican priests in Ireland didn't agree with. The Roman Catholic faith remained rooted in Ireland. The English Protestants who came to settle in Ireland were common soldiers who soon realized they had no prospect in new, foreign land. They decided it was easier to sell the small plots of land given to them and return to England. Those who remained were officers who received large amounts of land that brought them decent revenues. When Oliver Cromwell died in 1658, his position as lord protector was assumed by his son, Richard, who was far less ambitious. Cromwell's passionate governmental officials were replaced with more accommodating men.

The Cromwellian government in England collapsed in 1660 when Charles Stuart (r. as Charles II 1660–85) returned from exile and assumed the throne. The restoration of the monarchy brought new hope to Ireland, where even the Protestants welcomed Charles's accession. They genuinely expected that the years of military and political turmoil were over. However, Ireland was still filled with resentment, and those whose property was confiscated still waited for reconciliation. In truth, they waited for their chance to get revenge.

Kingdom Restored

In 1662, Charles II appointed James Butler, the Earl of Ormond, as the new lord-lieutenant of Ireland. He already served this post in the 1640s, under the reign of Charles I. He was a Protestant from an Old English family who tried to reach an agreement with the Catholics during his previous service in Ireland. But when Charles was overthrown, Buttler followed his king into exile. Once again in the position, he sought to reverse the Cromwellian land settlement. First, he compelled the Protestants to give up a third of their lands. Then he set up courts in which the Catholics had to prove they took no part in the insurrections of the 1640s to be given portions of their land back. But the recovery of the land in such a way was very slow, and in the end, no one was completely satisfied. The Cromwellians were angry they had to give up parts of their land, while the Catholics lacked the means to prove their innocence. In 1641, the Catholics owned three-fifths of the total Irish agricultural land. By the late 1660s, they owned only one-fifth. Ormond and Charles II played with the thought of a radical redistribution scheme, but in the end, they gave up out of fear they would provoke Protestants and Parliament. Unsatisfied Catholics formed bands and took to the hills and woods, raiding the newly-established Protestant settlements. These bands would persist throughout the 17th century as an important lawless element of Irish history. Some of them would even become national heroes.

The Catholics had more luck in matters of religion. Ormond was willing to allow them to practice Roman Catholicism if they would sign a declaration recognizing royal authority and denouncing the pope's ability to depose the king. Of course, these terms were unacceptable to the Catholic Church because denouncing any of the papal rights would mean denouncing the head of their religion. But for the most part, Catholics were left alone to practice their faith even if they refused to sign this declaration. The Cromwellian persecution of Catholics had finally ended. A Declaration of Indulgence from 1672 brought the end of the laws that imposed penalties on Catholics and their priests. Catholic exiles on the continent returned, and the clergy started restoring the church's infrastructure and hierarchy.

But some of the members of the House of Commons back in London were outraged by the actions of the Catholics. In 1673, they declared that the Declaration of Indulgence was invalid. They also introduced a Test Act, which required all officeholders to take communion in an established state church. By October of the same year, all Catholic priests and clergymen were once again ordered to leave Ireland or face the consequences. Although the measures were not as firmly enforced as during Cromwell's time, the fear was imposed upon Catholics, and many left willingly. The situation escalated during the late 1670s when the alleged Catholic plot to murder King Charles II was rumored. In Ireland, hundreds of Catholics were arrested and imprisoned, but when the rumor was exposed to be a lie, they were released, and Ireland lived in relative peace for the remainder of Charles's reign.

By 1685, Ireland's population swelled to two million. Two-thirds were Catholics, mostly native Irish who were predominantly an agricultural labor force. Among them were also evicted landlords who were compensated with a small plot in Connacht. There, they formed a small core of Catholic gentry, lawyers, and merchants. They formed a force that would organize and lead a Catholic resurgence if the occasion presented itself. And it did present itself in 1685 with the accession of James II (r. 1685–1688), the last Catholic monarch on the English throne. Under his reign, Richard Talbot (1630–1691) rose to power, first as Earl of Tyrconnell and commander in chief in Ireland (1685) and then as lord-lieutenant (1687). He was the first Catholic lord-lieutenant in more than one hundred years, and he was eager to restore Catholic men to the governmental offices in Ireland. He also started raising a Catholic army for the king to defend Parliament from angry Protestants, as he wanted to overthrow the Cromwellian settlement.

But the Catholic hopes of overthrowing the settlement were short-lived. King James's obvious favoritism of Catholics angered the Protestants both in Ireland and in England. They decided to offer the English crown to Prince William of Orange (1650–1702), the Duch ruler who was married to James's daughter, Mary. She was a Stuart, and as such, she guaranteed the stability of the dynasty. But she was also a Protestant. When James got a son in 1677, the prospect of the Catholic dynasty became very real to the Protestants, and seven English nobles sent an official invitation to William to come and overthrow his father-in-law and take the crown. But the Dutch ruler obliged them only in 1688, when he landed at Torbay in Devonshire with a large army. He marched to take London in the "Glorious Revolution" of 1688, forcing James to depart for France. The Duch couple now occupied the English throne, and the Catholics of Ireland were left to Protestant mercy.

However, Tyrconnell remained in Ireland, and he maintained connections with the exiled king. He was the last hope of the Catholics, and the Protestants feared him. Across Ireland, the Protestants were preparing for armed resistance. Exiled James came to Ireland in 1689, bringing money and troops from France. He then traveled to Dublin, where he summoned the Catholic Parliament. Together, they worked on reversing the Cromwellian land settlement. Catholics regarded this parliament as a triumph of freedom and resistance, but the Protestants saw it as an assembly created to deprive them of all possessions in Ireland. But James refused to officially abolish the Protestant Church of Ireland and Poynings' Law, which required royal approval of all acts of the Irish Parliament. In the eyes of his Catholic subjects, he had failed to uphold his promises.

William of Orange, ruling England as William III, sent his troops to Ireland in 1690. The two armies met near Dublin, and the River Boyne was used as a defense line by the Catholic troops of King James. On July 1, 1690, the Battle of the Boyne took place. James's armies failed to defend the city, and Dublin fell to William. James had no other choice but to once more flee to France. But his forces were determined to defend the Catholic estates to the west of Dublin, and they retreated to the River Shannon. They fought a resistance and were successful in their intention to preserve the estates. But Tyrconnell followed his king, and he took all the French troops with him. William returned to England, but his troops managed to cross the Shannon in 1691. On July 12, 1691, the decisive battle occurred at the field at Aughrim in County Galway. Just when it looked like William's troops were defeated, they rallied and inflicted a heavy blow to the Catholics. Limerick fell in August, signaling the end of the Catholic struggle. Tyrconnell returned, but without promised help from France, and he died just before the fall of Limerick. With his death, the Irish saw no point in fighting. On October 3, 1691, the Treaty of Limerick was signed, granting liberty to all Irish soldiers who took part in the fighting to go to France. Those who stayed could retain their properties; they were also given the freedom to practice their professions and the religious freedoms they possessed under the rule of Charles II. The lands of those who went to France were confiscated. More than 14,000 soldiers decided to go to the continent, where France fought Anglo-Dutch forces. In a way, they continued their struggle and remained known in history as "Wild Geese," Irish soldiers that distinguished themselves in European wars of the 18th century.

Chapter 6 – The Protestant Ascendancy

Royal Standard of Kingdom of Ireland

https://en.wikipedia.org/wiki/Protestant_Ascendancy#/media/
File:Royal_Standard_of_Ireland_(1542%E2%80%931801).svg

The Triumphant English Protestants remained in Ireland to consolidate and secure their control over the island. The governing system that came out as the product of their victory is known as the "Ascendancy" or the "Protestant Ascendancy." The term itself was coined in 1792 by Orangeman John Giffard, editor of Faulkner's *Dublin Journal*, but it refers to the whole 18th, 19th, and beginning of the 20th century. It labels a period in which the Protestants of the Church of Ireland exercised total control over Ireland and its society. They were subjects only to the Crown of Great Britain (its new title in 1707 after the union of England and Scotland) and to the English Parliament. During the period of Ascendancy, the Protestants created an elite and exclusive world in Ireland whose legacy is still visible in the city of Dublin, which they completely rebuilt.

During the Ascendancy period, two distinct societies emerged: a minority Protestant society and the Catholics, who composed most of the Irish population. The Protestants were the privileged layer of society, while Catholics suffered under their oppression. The Ascendency depended largely on exercising the Penal Laws, as it was constantly under the threat of Roman Catholicism. Penal Laws were legislation that effectively disabled the Catholics from exercising any political or social influence and power. The 18th century was one of the longest periods of peace in Irish history, and the country managed to achieve a degree of prosperity. Nevertheless, this prosperity was very limited because Great Britain limited Ireland's access to transatlantic trade. But at the end of the 18th century, the political ties between Ireland and the Crown started weakening. Influenced by the democratic movements in America, some of the Protestant elite in Ireland started pushing for political changes. They were angered by the economic limitations imposed on them by Great Britain, and they were proud of Ireland's turbulent history. The Irish Parliament decided that the interests of its own country were separate from those of Great Britain. For the first time in the history of Ireland, the Protestants and the Catholics were united with the same goal. The Protestant Whig Party joined the Catholic Committee in a call for reform. In the streets, Protestant volunteers joined forces with the Catholic Defenders, ready to take arms against the Crown. The Irish

Parliament secured its virtual independence, and the Catholics finally won relaxation of the measures taken against them.

But the limited success of these initial requirements for freedom bolstered the people, and the Irish started demanding even more radical actions. In 1798, the Society of United Irishmen and the Catholics rose in rebellion against Protestant predominance. They wanted to create an independent Irish republic by instigating a revolution modeled after those of America and France. However, they failed, and their defeat meant the loss of the institutional separatism of Ireland. The Irish Parliament ceased to exist, and at the turn of the 19th century, union with Great Britain was decreed. This was not the end of the Irish national hopes, and the people would continue their fight throughout the centuries, but their voices were often silenced as the Crown dealt with concerns of worldwide dimensions.

The Society of Ireland in 18th Century

Even though Catholics composed most of Ireland's population, numbering around two million at the end of the 17th century, they mostly occupied rural regions and were completely devoid of leadership. Most of the prominent Catholic families who fought against the English Parliament were either killed in the battle or had fled the country with the given opportunity. Most people lived as their Irish ancestors did by holding to the land they farmed in communal possession. They paid the rent in kind rather than money, and they rarely involved themselves in trade outside their immediate markets. They were just as poor as peasants anywhere else in Europe. But, unlike their European counterparts, the Irish people were ruled by those who were completely different from them, ethnically and religiously.

In the 18th century, the elite of the Irish society was comprised mostly of the new English settlers, together with some of the descendants of the first English colonists who converted to Protestantism during the reign of Elizabeth I. Among them were also landowners of Scottish descent, although they remained concentrated in Ulster. The minorities among them were the old Anglo-Irish and Gaelic Irish lords who converted to English ways and started marrying into English families. All of them were Protestants and members of the Anglican Church of Ireland. Only the Ulster-Scots were Presbyterians, but they were considered a nonconformist Protestant sect. As such, the entirety of the Irish elite upheld the English commercial, legal, and political systems. Cromwellian conquests seemed to continue, and Parliament abolished the *clachan* settlements of the Irish natives. These settlements were forced to knock down their walls and fences, and since they no longer owned their land, they had to pay rent to the landowners.

During the 18th century, the Irish landlords numbered around 10,000 families, and only a hundred or so of them were magnates, owning most of the fertile land of Ireland. Some of the parcels were reserved for the church and thus out of their reach, but these were small territories anyway. These magnates were the ones who dictated the political system of the country. But to actively participate in politics, one had to possess a city residency. So, the magnates moved from their vast estates in the countryside to the city of Dublin, and its development exploded. Throughout the century, the city expanded. At the turn of the 19th century, it numbered 180,000 inhabitants. The residing elites were the ones who ran the politics, but they also promoted commercial growth.

The religious, ethnic, and cultural divide between the Protestant minority and the Irish Catholic majority was a reality in everyday life. Stereotypes grew on both sides of the divide. The Irish thought of their English lords as arrogant, greedy, cunning, and intolerant. The English, on the other hand, thought of the Irish as lazy, ignorant, and superstitious. Many ethnic Irish chose to remain in the territories predominantly occupied by the Protestants. Although they merged into Protestant society, learned the language, and practiced English customs, they retained knowledge of the Irish language and often acted as patrons of Irish poets, artists, and priests. These artists and priests were former members of the old Irish society that had lost their status. Resenting the English dominance, they fabricated stories of a former Irish golden age and great ancestry and fed the Irish Catholics these myths. Through these stories, the common folk became persuaded that they had been unjustly deprived of their property, and they were determined to get it all back. But during the 18th century, the Catholics had no means with which they could recover their lost properties and the dignity of their great ancient nation. They could only hope and dream.

The Penal Laws

Although the Protestants had defeated the Irish under the leadership of King William III, fear of the Catholics remained. To the Protestants, the speed with which the Catholics regained power in 1685 and 1689 was proof that Protestant authority wasn't secure. The Nine Years' War with France still raged, and many Irish soldiers were fighting on the French side. They were a threat to the Irish Protestants, who feared their enemies would come back from the continent as an invasion force. To maintain their supremacy, the Protestants took measures to contain the Catholics. The Irish Parliament was entirely composed of Protestant members, who set about legislating a complex series of Penal Laws to formally exclude Catholics from participating in any public affairs. Parliament called Catholic lords "the papist gentlemen," and at the end of the 17th century, they forbade them to carry arms for self-defense or for hunting. Anyone who sought to hold office in the army, navy, or administration had to swear an oath denying the doctrine of transubstantiation (conversion of bread and wine into the body and blood of Christ). Catholics declined to swear such oaths, so entry to these careers was denied them. But this wasn't enough. The Protestants also wanted to keep the Catholics from acquiring land.

From 1703–1704 and again in 1709, they came up with property bills that stated that Catholics could not lease land for longer than thirty-one years, and they were no longer able to buy it. In 1729, the Catholics lost the right to vote for members of Parliament.

Catholics constituted around 75 percent of the whole Irish population in the 1770s, but they owned only 5 percent of the territory of the island. Denied the right to own land, they quickly lost wealth. As if that wasn't enough to make them suffer, the Irish Parliament ordered them to pay tithes to the Anglican Church of Ireland. In subsequent years, laws were passed which proscribed Catholic worship, teaching, religious organizations, and practices such as pilgrimage and procession. Protestant missionaries went all over the country promoting conversion and opening charter schools which, in 1746, were given government grants. But these missionaries achieved little because Catholics remained distrustful. Also, the Protestant elite needed to stay a small, separate ruling body to keep their privileged status, so the conversion of the masses was done half-heartedly. They were even strict with nonconformist sects such as Presbyterians. Even though non-Anglican Protestants enjoyed property rights and were granted legal religious tolerance in 1719, they too were excluded from royal offices and had to pay tithes to the established church. To keep their social positions, some of the remaining Catholic landowners, barristers, and lawyers converted, but most of the people remained Catholic.

The Irish Parliament was in no way a democratic body; the landed aristocrats and the Church of Ireland held all the power in their hands. To be chosen as a member of the Parliament, aside from being Protestant, one had to have certain income and property qualifications. Only the wealthiest of the elite were eligible for Parliament. Since only a handful of voters existed, voting turned into a mere formality. The English Parliament won certain powers during the Glorious Revolution, but none of them applied to Ireland. In England, Parliament members changed every few years, whereas in Ireland, one could hold a position for life. In Ireland, a new Parliament had to be elected only if and when the monarch died. The Irish Parliament met every two years to appropriate additional revenues because the hereditary revenues received by the government never covered public expenses. Part of the government's revenues was set aside for the maintenance of a large army. In fact, in the 18th century, Ireland had an army twice the size of that in Britain. It was stationed in the countryside, where the need to quell an occasional uprising grew.

The final authority resided in the government of England. No legislation could be passed without royal approval. Aside from appointing the lord-lieutenant of Ireland, the British government created the office of the chief secretary, who served as a spokesman of the British administration before the Irish House of Commons. His opinions were greatly important, and during the 18th century, the importance of this office grew significantly. Both lord-lieutenant and chief secretary worked in the interests of the English government, not Ireland. But they only needed to be present in Ireland when Parliament would meet, once every two years. This meant they were mostly absent, and political figures known as the "Undertakers" undertook the promotion of the government's agenda. They used patronage to promote voting for the interests of the English government. Because the Irish Parliament completely depended on the will of the monarch and the English Parliament, it was often threatened with the loosening of the restraints on Catholics.

But some of the Penal Laws quickly fell into disuse even without the intervention of the English Parliament. For example, the law that forbade Catholics from carrying weapons or owning a horse that was worth no more than five pounds quickly fell into disuse. Because most of the Irish population was Catholic, it became clear it would be impossible to regulate their private lives. The Catholic priests who were permitted to stay were the core of the leadership of the church that gradually recovered its strength. At the beginning of the century, masses were held outside, in the open, and in hiding. But during the 1750s, priests regained their rights to hold indoor masses for their followers and even started their training programs in Ireland. But the Catholic Church could not bear the label of a church that was reserved to the buildings of the established faith. Instead, Catholic priests held masses in barns, storehouses, and even in open fields. These places were called chapels, and they could be found everywhere across Ireland, tucked away in the quiet alleys of the cities or towns and scattered all over the countryside landscape.

Because the papacy continued to support the Stuart dynasty until 1766, all Catholics in Ireland were considered disloyal to the Crown. But mid-century, a Catholic party that claimed that not all Catholics were inherently disloyal started to emerge. These Catholics even addressed loyalty petitions to the king during the Seven Years' War with France, and the government considered forming a Catholic regiment that would be sent to fight in Portugal, Spain, France, and Austria. But the time wasn't yet ripe. As Parliament prepared to introduce bills by which they would allow Catholics mortgages to obtain property in Munster and Ulster, a rebellion broke out. Pressed by the tithes, unemployment, and high rent they could not address in the court, society took arms. The rebels were not only Catholics but secret societies of Protestants (namely the Hearts of Oak and the Hearts of Steel) who also could not afford rent. These were joined by the Catholic agrarian societies, including the Rightboys and the Whiteboys or Levellers (*Buachaillí Bána*). But these uprisings of the 1760s were short-lived and only served to give the government a reason to ban such disturbances. Nevertheless, the government failed to address the resentment the people felt, and in the next decade, political agitation added to the discontent.

Years of Discontent in Ireland

From 1740 to 1815, Britain was constantly at war. It had a growing need for agricultural products and textiles to supply its army. Aside from the army, Britain needed to feed and clothe its growing population, and, for that, it needed Irish production. During the middle 18th century, the economy in Ireland grew rapidly, and with it came the growth of income, consumption, and output. The number of landlords increased, as the British were buying properties in Ireland with low-interest rates, but they were mainly absent lords who lived in Britain. All their revenue from Ireland was sent to their homeland, leaving the labor population to starve. The economic growth was felt by the aristocracy, but not the population. Life was insecure for commoners, but the population grew steadily. The sudden population boom had consequences, such as higher rent, shorter leases, and the prohibition of subletting. Catholics taught that the Protestants were exploiting them, but the Protestants, too, were unsatisfied with the governmental restriction on trade and their limited rights to get involved in government. At this point, the people in the American colonies were stirring, demanding independence, and in 1775, they finally took up arms. The Irish people sympathized with American rebels and thought that many aspects of the situation in the colonies were similar to their sufferings. In Ireland, anti-government sentiment surged, and the people started calling for radical action.

In 1760, in Dublin, the Irish Patriot Party of parliamentarians started opposing the government. They formed an alliance with MPs (Members of Parliament) in England, the Whigs who opposed the ruling Tories. In the British capital, the opposition was led by Edmund Burke, who was born in Dublin but in the 1750s had moved to London, where he became a member of the British Parliament. He entered the House of Commons in 1765 as a member of the Whig Party, and he centered his career on the assertion of parliamentary rights and defense of the rights of the

American colonists. When the war in America started, taxes were raised in Ireland to finance the British army. Aggravated by high taxes, the Patriot MPs in Dublin called for a declaration of rights. However, their definition of Patriotism was very narrow, favoring the Protestant elite instead of national interests. The declaration of rights would give Dublin's Parliament a legal guarantee of legislative and judiciary independence. It would mean that the Irish Parliament wouldn't need to wait for royal approval and legislation to pass in the English Parliament before they could adopt it. The leader of the Patriot Party was Henry Flood, an MP from Kilkenny, but he accepted a government office in 1775, passing the leadership to Henry Grattan. With his extraordinary oratorical skills, Grattan immediately became the spokesman of the Irish House of Commons.

Grattan was very passionate about the nationhood of Ireland, but he understood the ties his country had with England were so deep that they could no longer be broken. In May of 1782, he gave his famous speech in which he declared that Ireland was connected to England not only by loyalty to the king but also by liberty. Ireland was linked with the constitutional liberties of Britain, and there was no denying that complete independence was impossible. The American war had dislocated trade and put additional weight on the economy of Ireland, which was already weakened by heavy taxation. Calls for the lift of trade restrictions were continuously made after 1775. When France and Spain entered the war in 1778/9, Ireland was left defenseless as Britain pulled all available soldiers to fight overseas. Irish Protestants organized a volunteer army. They had no uniforms and were sponsored by local magnates who needed their estates to be protected. This meant that the public had control of the only army in Ireland, while the government had none. Members of the opposition quickly took advantage of this fact and started commandeering the volunteer army. Once again, on November 4, 1779, the Irish demanded the removal of trade restrictions, but the campaign reached its climax only in February of 1782 when the Ulster volunteers gathered to adopt a resolution of legislative and judicial independence and the relaxation of the Penal Laws. The British government, still fighting the war in America and now suffering the threats of the Irish people, felt extremely pressured.

The officials in London didn't know how to respond, and the government led by Lord North fell from power in 1782. Whigs replaced the Tory ministers, and they were anxious to appease the Irish population. In January of 1782, the Tories repealed the Declaratory Act and altered the Poynings' Law to allow the bills approved by the Irish Parliament to reach London unaltered. On April 17, 1783, the British Parliament passed the British Renunciation Act, by which it renounced its right to legislate for Ireland. All remaining restrictions on Irish trade were also removed. Ireland thus became an independent kingdom in every way, but it shared Britain's monarch. The foundation of the national bank and separate post office followed in 1783, and in 1786, Dublin founded its police force. Feelings of national unity spread, and in the spirit of reconciliation, the Protestants lifted many property restrictions previously imposed on Catholics. But the political reality soon hit Ireland. The Irish Parliament gained its independence and was legally separate from the British, but Ireland remained largely under British control. The king still appointed the lord-lieutenant of Ireland to act as the British governmental representative. Through the lord-lieutenant, the British government controlled and selected the Irish officials, though not directly—they only had control over their salaries and pensions, as well as the power to appoint people to the offices. With this power, the government still influenced the Irish MPs. Among them, reformers pushed for greater changes, but most of the landed gentry was satisfied with the outcome of the British Renunciation Act.

The Revolutionary Sentiment in Ireland

In May of 1789, France overthrew its monarchy. The Bourbon dynasty went down in revolution, and a republic was installed. Past politics were cast aside, and society started rebuilding itself. The ripples of these events reached Ireland very fast since the two countries shared commerce, culture, and religion. In Ireland, people started calling for reducing the privileges of the aristocracy and ending discrimination. Democracy started shaping itself slowly, and the comfortable world of the Ascendancy aristocrats was coming to an end. The Irish Parliament and the Whigs were still led by Grattan, and they now demanded the purification of Parliament by limiting the number of officeholders who were sitting in the legislative body. Whig clubs were formed in two Irish cities: in Dublin in 1789 and in Belfast in 1790. They promoted parliamentary reforms and organized opposition to the legislative unions of Ireland.

The segment of Ireland's population that was stirred by the American revolution now found a new reason to call for democratic changes within the country: they were frustrated by the inability and unwillingness of the Patriot MPs to promote reform. Young Protestant barristers from Dublin launched a movement based on the model of the French Revolution, which sparked interest among the Presbyterian bourgeoisie in Ulster. They thought that the ruling Anglican landlords were limiting their economic interests and pushed for reforms. Among those who started the movement was Theobald Wolfe Tone. In 1791, he was called to Belfast to address the Presbyterian activists. He attracted their attention by publishing "An Argument on Behalf of the Catholics of Ireland" in 1791. In this work, Tone called for the unification of Catholics and Protestants because only united would the two factions be strong enough to push for changes. He didn't believe in religious equality, and he thought of Roman Catholicism as a dying faith that would soon become only a distant memory. But for now, he needed the two factions to work together to reform Parliament and secure the complete independence of Ireland. For more than two weeks, negotiations and debates took place. The result was the creation of the Belfast Society of United Irishmen on October 14, 1791. Inspired by Tone's efforts, his friend, James Napper Tandy, founded a branch of this society in Dublin.

The United Irishmen represented middle-class radical Protestants, most of its members Presbyterians. Their main goal was to use the pressure of public opinion to force the government to accept changes. But they were not alone. Soon, they were joined by the political clubs and volunteer corps, who passed a resolution of solidarity with the United Irishmen. Inspired by the efforts of their countrymen, Catholics started demanding changes too. A Catholic Committee, which had existed since 1760, remained largely elitist in its membership and conservative in its program. But the increased revolutionary sentiment of the early 1790s made it accept more radical ideas. In 1791, the committee presented King George III with a petition that asked for relief for his Catholic subjects in Ireland. But, to ensure the Protestants were on the same page, the Catholics employed Protestant Theobald Wolfe Tone as their chief secretary. They hoped this gesture would prove their commitment to religious tolerance.

In December of 1793, Catholics from all over Ireland met in Tailors Hall in Dublin, where they agreed their main goal was the abolition of the remaining Penal Laws. They bypassed the lord-lieutenant by sending a delegation to London, where they were received with sympathies. The British government was always afraid that by emancipating the Irish Catholics, the Irish Parliament would change in such a manner that an Irish break from Great Britain would be imminent. However, at this point, Britain was again facing a war with France, and it had to consider the situation with international interests in mind. The government wanted to appease Irish public opinion, and in 1793, the Relief Act was passed in the

Dublin legislature, which removed the remaining laws against Catholics. However, the Catholics were still barred from entering civil service, could not be elected as parliamentarians, and could not be appointed in judicial offices. They could, however, marry Protestants, buy and sell land without restrictions, and practice at the bar. The same year, the first Catholic higher education institution, St. Patrick's College, was opened.

The fact that Catholics were now allowed to buy and sell land led to increased tensions between them and the Protestants, mainly in south Ulster, where they resided in equal numbers. There, the "Defenders" were formed, a Catholic secret society that was heavily influenced by the French revolutionists. Their goal was to "quell all nations, dethrone all kings, and plant the true religion that was lost at the Reformation" (Newman 1991, 47). In the mid-1790s, their ideology started spreading to the artisans in towns, who were suffering increased taxes. The Defenders inspired the Protestants to start their own opposing secret society known as the "Peep o'Day Boys." When the Defenders wanted to hold armed demonstrations, the Peep o'Day Boys fought them in what became known as the Battle of the Diamond. The fighting started near Loughgall in the County of Armagh on September 21, 1795. The battle itself was very short, and the Defenders suffered only thirty deaths, but this information is based on hearsay. According to witnesses, the Peep o'Day Boys had no casualties at all. The effect of this battle was the foundation of the Loyal Orange Institution, or the Orange Order, a Protestant organization sworn to protect the king and his family so long as he supported the Protestant Ascendancy. Members of this organization soon appeared all over Ulster.

In the meantime, the Parliament under Garret's leadership sought to gain even more freedoms for the Catholics. In 1795, the Irish Parliament proposed the complete emancipation of the Catholics. But this was too soon, as it only served to convince the British government of Ireland's separatist intentions. Britain set out to crush this sentiment for independence. However, it had nearly no means to do so. The regular troops were fighting the French, so the government was forced to set up a militia. Although this militia had been in place since 1793, the government had to do excessive recruiting. But the political loyalty of the swelling numbers of the militia couldn't be guaranteed. The ranks were filled with poor Catholic peasants who were, in reality, controlled by the Defenders. In 1796, Lord-lieutenant John Jeffreys Pratt (1759–1840) felt he needed to found a separate division of militia consisting solely of Protestants as a counterbalance to the Catholic members. They were known as the Yeomanry Corps, and they numbered thousands of Protestants.

The government needed to crack down on the Irish revolutionary spirit because it didn't want a weak monarchy while at war with France. The authorities suppressed the Dublin Society of United Irishmen, and in 1796, the British Parliament passed an act by which officials had wide powers to search for arms and impose a curfew in the troubled areas. The Dublin United Irishmen had to go underground, but this only made it a more ruthless and much tougher organization. Tone was still active, and he now called for a complete break from Great Britain. The Catholic Defenders and the United Irishmen movements drew closer together, as they were both advocating the complete emancipation of Catholics and constitutional reform. In some areas, they even merged completely. The term "constitutional reform" now meant the establishment of a republic modeled after America and France. The government would be completely independent of Britain.

But the government had its supporters in the Orange Order, other Protestant societies, and in Yeomanry militia. They were all determined to uphold law and order in Ireland and keep the island connected to Great Britain. The British government was aware of the possibility of a French invasion, even more so when Wolfe Tone went there to ask for assistance. Tone spoke to the French government, promising Ireland would welcome its intervention, but the French didn't need much persuasion. The French government wanted to take over the Irish ports and disable much of British trade—the trade that allowed Britain to become an active opponent of French ambitions as a republic and European superpower. In December of 1796, the French fleet set sail for Ireland under the command of General Louis-Lazare Hoche (1768–97). But since they had started their journey mid-winter, they met heavy storms at sea and were forced to turn back. Nevertheless, Ireland was swelling with discontent, and the Ascendancy politicians were afraid that revolution would start anytime.

In 1797, the government decided to purge the United Irishmen from the ranks of the militia. Afraid the government would gain the initiative by this action, the Irishmen decided to attack. Together with their allies, the Defenders, they planned an uprising for the summer of 1798, but before it could happen, the government arrested the leaders of the Leinster provincial branch of the movement. On March 30, Lord Camden issued a proclamation claiming that the country was in a state of rebellion and effectively imposed martial law. The movement continued with its planned attacks, with the first insurrections breaking out in May and June of 1798, but they were badly coordinated. They never managed to grow and become anything but localized, isolated skirmishes. By June 13, the armed insurrections in Ulster ended when the activists suffered a defeat at Ballynahinch. The members of the United Irishmen were slaughtered as they were trying to flee. Two days later, their leader, Henry Munro, was executed.

The rebels had their greatest success in Wexford, where they managed to march triumphantly into town on May 31. Many more battles ensued, and the rebels suffered great defeats and massacres. The most notable ones were on June 5 at New Ross and on June 21 at Vinegar Hill. More than 30,000 insurgents lost their lives, and the rebellion ended at the start of the summer. The remaining Irish rebels looked to France for help but were greatly disappointed. France's new commander, Napoleon Bonaparte (1769–1821), was about to start his Egyptian conquest and could divert only a minor squadron to help Ireland. They arrived in August and were too late to help with the rebellion. Upon their arrival, the French officers, hardened during the French Revolution, were surprised at how poorly the Irishmen were equipped. Nevertheless, they offered their assistance and, on August 27, defeated the Yeomanry at Castlebar. They also set up the Republic of Connacht but were surrounded by the British forces and had to surrender by September. The French were given safe passage back to their own county, but the Irish rebels were executed. Wolfe Tone went back to France, where he served as adjutant general. But on October 12, his vessel, the *Hoche*, was captured by a British squadron. It was a minor engagement, but the British were very pleased to capture Tone. He was tried by court-martial and sentenced to the gallows. But, on November 19, Wolfe Tone died of a neck wound, presumably self-inflicted.

The Rebellion of 1798 ended, and the Irish aspirations for self-rule had failed again. Nevertheless, Catholics were still the majority, and among the common people, nationalist sympathies were on the rise. The memory of the "Ninety-Eight" rebellion burned in the minds of later generations. A whole new mythology was weaved around the events of that spring and summer, and new ballads such as "The Memory of the Dead," "The Wearin o' the Green," "The Boys of Wexford," and many others continued to tell the stories. Later generations would draw inspiration from these songs and battle with a determination equal to that of their ancestors. But the political scene of Great Britain would be completely different.

The fact that Ireland could raise a rebellion meant that the island was out of British control and needed to be put back in the firm grasp of the monarchy. To this end, British Prime Minister William Pitt the Younger (1759–1806) proposed the merging of the two parliaments, the Irish and the British. He argued that if the two legislatures were to come together, the Protestant fear of Catholic emancipation would come to an end because, within Great Britain, the Catholics would become a minority. Pitt's scheme was a rational one, and he continued to persuade his colleagues by adding that one parliament would be more efficient and would promote British investment in the Irish economy. The united government would bring an end to local sentiments, as the interests of the whole monarchy would prevail. But many Irish MPs, even though they were against rebellion, committed to maintaining a separate identity. Still led by Grattan, they mounted a defense of Irish national individuality. They claimed they needed their own parliament to give the nation its own political voice. In 1799, Grattan's MPs held many loud debates and managed to defeat the proposal to unify the two parliaments. However, this victory was very small, as they won by only five votes. This encouraged the government to organize propaganda and persuasion by bribery. In June of 1800, the Act of Union passed, and in August, royal approval was granted. Ireland became part of the United Kingdom in January of 1801.

Chapter 7 – The Act of Union and the Great Famine

A memorial to the Great Famine in Dublin

https://en.wikipedia.org/wiki/Great_Famine_(Ireland)#/media/
File:Famine_memorial_dublin.jpg

In 1801, Ireland's Parliament voted itself out of existence. All political debates and decisions were to be made in London. The fate of the whole island was now in the hands of the faraway legislature, but an opposition had already formed. It presented itself in resurgent Catholic nationalism, which arose in the early 19th century. The Catholics of all classes united to fight for complete emancipation, and their drive was led by a single politician, Daniel O'Connell (1775-1847). He dominated Irish political life in the first half of the 19th century with his massive, non-violent campaigns challenging the governmental system. He focused on newly-found national pride among Ireland's majority population, the Catholics, but he also appealed to the young of any faction, as he saw the new generations' ability to supply fresh ideas to advance the Irish cause.

But while O'Connell preached and practiced pacifist tactics, Ireland was going through the most troubling times. The nightmarish reality of mass starvation and disease pandemics grasped the island. The potato blight and the Great Famine shook western Europe and changed Ireland profoundly. Thousands died, millions migrated, and Ireland experienced the most tragic mass depopulation in history. Irish men, women, and children were forced to flee for their lives. But the famine had unexpected consequences. It hardened the attitudes and actions of the young Irish, who switched their tactics from pacifist methods of persuasion to a swift, violent blow to British rule. The British government failed to combat the famine, and this failure was the last drop in the ocean of grievances that the Irish had been harboring for so long.

Ireland and the Society of 19th Century

The 19th century in Ireland began with an entirely new political scene, but the main governmental players had hardly changed. The union with Great Britain left Irish affairs in the hands of 658 members of the House of Commons, of which only around one hundred were Irish. The concerns the Irish had would be forced to compete for the government's attention. But the Irish lawmakers who sat in the British Parliament and those back home who executed the law remained the same people as before. The Ascendancy still prevailed, and the Protestants ran the public administration from Dublin. When Ireland entered the union, it was greatly divided, but it was no longer only the division between Protestants and Catholics: Protestants were divided between those with rebel sentiments and those who supported the government. Landlords and the Anglican clergy preferred the union because it safeguarded the continuation of their dominance. Protestant peasants and the working class, as well as Presbyterians, opposed the union because they thought the British government would be inclined to give more equality to the Catholics.

In 1803, the last echo of the 1798 rebellion could be felt in the shape of a small, localized uprising. The United Irishmen, led by Robert Emmet (1778–1803), made plans to seize Dublin Castle. They still hoped France would come to their assistance, although no help came. Nevertheless, on July 23, a brief scuffle occurred on the streets of Dublin in which chief justice Lord Kilwarden and his son-in-law were stabbed to death. Robert Emmet was quickly captured and executed, joining the pantheon of Irish freedom fighters. But Irish Catholics were possibly even more politically divided than Irish Protestants. As the Catholic peasants remained resentful towards the Protestants and the British government for centuries of oppression, middle-class Catholics were willing to work in the new system imposed by the Act of Union to make a better living standard for themselves. Their main hope was to gain equal political rights within the British government, and that would open to them the capitalist world in which they could prosper. Many Catholic laymen and clergy denounced the rebellion of 1798 and now supported the union. But profound changes in Irish society would occur during the 19th century, and these Catholics who supported the union would again change their minds.

The economic depression that set in after the Napoleonic Wars ended in 1815 tied all Protestants to the British government because it allowed them to enjoy protective tariffs and trade preferences. The Catholic competition for wages and leases pushed lower-class Protestants to seek the protection of the imperial government and their landlords. The Orange Order now represented institutionalized loyalty to imperial Great Britain. The order united lower and upper classes of Protestant society in a sectarian alliance which guaranteed Protestant prerogatives through the Act of Union. During the 1820s, the Orange Order swelled in numbers. By the mid 19th century, the order strengthened even more when middle-class Presbyterians started joining. Efforts to convert Catholics were renewed in this period, but just like the previous campaigns, they failed. However, this failure only served to deepen the Protestant prejudice towards Catholics.

In the early 19th century, education for Catholic children was prohibited, and many hedge schools appeared. They were designed to secretly bring education to Catholic children, who would gather in private homes. The teachers were often poorly qualified, but they taught Irish history and classical literature. During the 1820s, the laws loosened up, and schools for Catholics could be legally opened. The classes were usually held in barns and cottages, as the government wouldn't provide Catholic teachers with anything more than textbooks. Since these were in English, Catholics had to learn the English language, and the Irish language fell out of educational use. In 1831, a nationwide primary education system was set up. Even the Catholics were included and given the equipment and classrooms they needed; the hedge schools and barn classrooms were no longer needed. By the turn of the 20th century, the Catholic Church ran around 9,000 schools, and they greatly reduced illiteracy among the Irish population.

The Protestants of the 19th century still represented a ruling minority in Ireland. They comprised the middle and upper classes of society as aristocratic landlords, and they held all the positions in law, finance, commerce, and industry. Protestant farmers could be found, but even they were privileged head tenants who held the best land. Catholics were still the majority all over Ireland—except in the northeast, where the Protestants prevailed. More than 80 percent of the total Irish population were Catholics, and they were almost all peasants, farmers, and workers. During the early 19th century, a new layer of the working class appeared, known as the "cottiers." Their numbers grew quickly, and by the 1850s, they were the majority among the rural laborers. Cottiers were simple workers who received a cabin and two acres of land, or even less. This was enough to graze one cow and grow some potatoes. In turn, the cottiers had to spend a set number of days laboring in the fields of their employer. Most of these laborers didn't handle any cash, and they had no leases. Their employers deducted a very expensive rent from their very small wages, keeping total control. This system ensured a reliable workforce, while the cottiers gained land just large enough for sustenance. But cottiers lived their lives constantly on the brink of existence. Still, they weren't the poorest layer of society. Beneath them were the landless laborers and tiny smallholders, the poorest of the poor, who represented one-half of the total rural population of Ireland.

Secret societies grew in rural Ireland in the first half of the 19th century. They were the successors to groups such as the Whiteboys and other similar societies of the previous century, associations of farmers and laborers bound together by a secret oath. The Whiteboys reappeared in Munster, and new ones such as the Rockites and the Terry Alts sprouted all over the country. The Defenders went underground after the revolution, but they had never ceased to exist. Now, they emerged again as the Ribbonmen. They were alternatively known as the Society of St. Patrick or the

Association of the Shamrock, and they had lodges all over Ireland. These secret societies and similar groups were motivated by various grievances such as high taxes, rents, tithes, and low wages. They were violent groups, and over this period, they grew not only in numbers but also in intensity. They would openly battle against the police, and it wasn't uncommon for them to assassinate certain landlords. At fairs and markets, they would battle the Orangemen, sending direct threats to all Protestants in Ireland. The hostility between the Protestants and the Catholics took an even worse turn during the 19th century.

Catholic Nationalism

When promoting the Act of the Union, Prime Minister William Pitt promised the complete emancipation of the Irish Catholics. However, the Crown and the Anglican Tory opposition proved too strong, and all plans of emancipation were abandoned. In 1821, King George IV (r. 1820–1830) visited Ireland, and hopes were raised again. He even appointed a new lord-lieutenant, Richard Wellesley (1760–1842), who was pro-emancipation. But the politicians in Westminster had no interest in showing any sympathy for the Catholics, and expectations for change again disappeared. Catholics were disbarred from holding any offices if they refused to swear Protestant oaths. In the army, Catholics were unable to serve a higher rank than a colonel. Catholics felt that they deserved more prospects in their careers, as well as the opportunity to take part in political decision-making. But there was no clear sign that the situation would change any time soon, and the resentment of the Catholics grew during the 19th century. The drive to win Catholic emancipation could succeed unless the Catholics were to organize themselves and attract wide appeal. In this spirit, the Catholic Association was founded in 1823 by Daniel O'Connell.

The Catholic Association was based on a different kind of premise. Instead of gathering well-to-do Catholics or focusing only on the poor, Daniel O'Connell founded an organization that accepted all Catholics, no matter their social status. To attract the masses, he used priests because they knew the people and were present everywhere; they could easily rally the masses. The clergy was happy to oblige because they were angry at the Protestants who pushed for the conversion of their people. Priests openly supported O'Connell's campaign of emancipation. O'Connell also introduced a membership fee for his organization, but it cost no more than a penny a month. This was such a low amount that all but the poorest could afford it. The fee was there only for its psychological effect: members were proud, knowing that they were contributing to a collective effort to bring change to Ireland. Thousands of Catholics joined, and the money collected wasn't a small amount. Penny by a penny, the Catholic Association became unmatched in numbers and wealth.

To further inspire his people, O'Connell organized huge gatherings that encouraged solidarity and unity. In the summer of 1826, general elections were held, and the Catholic priests rallied the electors to lead them to the polls. Most of the voters were tenant farmers, and they managed to overturn the elections in Wexford, Westmeath, Lough, and Monaghan. The MP's they chose were Protestants, but ones sympathetic to the Catholic pleas. But the event that brought a turnabout in the minds of the British politicians occurred two years later, in 1828, when an MP for Clare resigned so he could accept office in the British Cabinet. Elections had to be held to elect a new MP for Clare, and although O'Donnell knew he couldn't sit in Parliament because he was a Catholic, no law would ban him from becoming a candidate. Again, priests shepherded the people to the voting places, and the result was O'Connell's victory, with 2,057 votes to 982. The government in Britain was shocked by these results. They were afraid that the Irish Catholics would be too excited by this victory and would resort to violence if the government declined it. They were aware of O'Donnell's non-violent methods, but who would guarantee peace once the Catholic masses were enraged? Besides, in the House of Commons, the majority favored emancipation. Prime Minister Arthur Wellesley and Home Secretary Robert Peel accepted the reality and brought the Catholic emancipation bill to the Parliament session in 1829. The bill turned into law in April of the same year, and the Catholics were now able to run for any governmental office except for the highest two—lord-lieutenant and lord chancellor of Ireland. O'Connell took his seat in Parliament, where he remained for the next twelve years and used his influence to support the Whig Party that was supportive of Irish causes.

Over the years, O'Connell worked to ensure that the Act of Union was repealed. In 1840, he organized the National Repeal Association, an organization that used the old and proven tactics of recruitment used by his Catholic Association. Again, a small membership fee was collected, and again, the clergy was used to rally the masses. O'Connell proclaimed 1843 as the "year of the repeal," and he held forty mass meetings in which he speeches to inspire the Catholics of Ireland. One such meeting entered the annals of history. It was held at Tara on August 15, 1843, and people from all over the country traveled for days to come and hear O'Connell speak. The leader of the National Repeal Association hoped public opinion would again sway the government, just as it did with the emancipation of the Catholics a decade earlier. But while emancipation had wide support in the House of Commons, not a single parliamentary supported the repeal except O'Connell and around twenty of his associates. The government was determined to keep the union, and the mass meetings of the National Repeal Association were banned. O'Connell retreated to Clontarf, and others took up leadership of the association. However, they were unable to decide which direction to take and how to organize the program, and the National Repeal Association slowly died out.

The peaceful power of mass gatherings and public opinion failed in the end, but its ideology continued and eventually brought victory. O'Connell managed to awaken the political consciousness of Irish Catholics, who were for so long excluded from decision-making. The people who were the majority in their own country were ruled by a minority precisely because they lacked the right of political expression. But now they had it, and they used it to spawn new patriotic associations that would use both peaceful and martial means to achieve the Irish right to self-govern. The Young Ireland movement consisted mostly of young, urban middle-class intellectuals, and many of them were even Protestants. They gathered around the weekly journal, *Nation*, which was founded in 1842 to help communicate O'Connell's ideas to the masses. Young Ireland sought to keep Irish nationalism alive in the people regardless of their social status or religious views. The movement didn't want to use violence in its fight for the independence of Ireland, but it remained open to that if the possibility presented itself. The leader of Young Ireland was Thomas Osborne Davis (1814–1845), and his national writings inspired many generations that came after. Although the movement resented using violence, they reverted to more radical measures when the economic hardship of the Great Famine pressed.

The Irish Potato Famine

Ireland had experienced potato harvest failures before. At least fourteen different blight cases occurred between 1816 and 1842, but what happened in 1845 had never been seen before. The new strain of blight was caused by a fungus known as *Phytophthora infestans*, which was imported from North America. It was incredibly virulent, spreading across the island in a matter of days. The leaves of the potato plants would first turn black and then crumbled into dust at the slightest touch. The blight started first in Scotland and Belgium in 1845 and quickly spread across northwestern Europe. But nowhere were people so dependent on the potato harvest as in Ireland. Desperate to save their fields, farmers tried cutting off the diseased leaves and stems, but the fungus affected the soil itself, and the potatoes were dying in the ground. Even the potatoes that looked healthy and edible would rot quickly after they were harvested.

The blight quickly encompassed half the island, and 30 to 40 percent of the harvest was destroyed. At first, only a few starved because the farmers reacted fast, selling their livestock and buying enough food to sustain their families. Also, the British government was fast to react, implementing a Poor Relief Act, a system that had been in place since 1838. Those who sought help from the state would have to enter the workhouses, institutions in which they were given food, a bed, and a job. The commissioners of the Poor Law were the ones who oversaw the system and accepted individuals or families into the workhouses. However, the Poor Relief Act wasn't enough, and the government soon recognized that famine would overwhelm the system. Wanted to avoid soaring food prices, they bought £100,000 of Indian corn and meals with which they hoped they could control the food market. Besides the Poor Law commissioners, the government also set up local committees tasked with distributing the food. The volunteers working with the most affected families were numerous, and the solidarity of the people greatly helped to avert starvation in 1845.

But the next year turned the threat of famine into a catastrophe. By August 1846, the blight spread through the entirety of Ireland and destroyed all its potato crops. Previously, in July, the Peels government had fallen and was replaced with the Whig ministry, which reduced the government relief efforts. Whigs largely ignored Irish affairs, as they believed the government should not meddle in the economic affairs of Great Britain. The new prime minister, Lord John Russell (1792-1878), left relief to the local workhouses and the buying and distributing of food to local merchants. His administration closed the food warehouses and suspended public work. Local relief committees were forbidden from selling food at lower prices than those on the market. Soon, the desperately poor Irishmen were unable to afford basic groceries. In some areas of the island, food was nowhere to be found.

The government soon realized the shortage of food was so serious that it had to launch a public work. However, the new laws required each local project to get approval from London, which created long delays. Thousands of people perished while waiting for approval or relief. When winter came, it proved to be one of the harshest ones in the history of Ireland. People panicked as hungry mobs roamed the countryside in search of anything that could sustain them for a little longer. The workhouses were swarmed, and the crowds only brought disease and rat infestation with them. In December of 1846, in Skibbereen (Country Cork), around one hundred bodies were found in a workhouse, half-eaten by rats. So many people died that the government was finally forced to re-implement the Poor Law. Around 2,000 relief committees were formed, and they distributed food to more than three million people around Ireland. But this was only 40 percent of the population. For the rest, the government had to rely on private initiatives such as charity and philanthropic societies. Irish Americans united and sent help, both food and money. The Religious Society of Friends (Quakers) opened soup kitchens around the country, but they also served as informants to communicate with people and direct them where they could get more specific help. They also spread the news of the severity of the famine in Ireland across the country and abroad. Both Catholic and Protestant religious groups offered help, but many Catholics had to convert to receive food from the Protestant relief groups. Landlords did everything they could do to hold to their riches, but a few of them had to proclaim bankruptcy as they spent their wealth to save their tenants from starvation.

The potato blight proved to be hard to deal with—it was constantly returning. The crops of 1846 were unusable, and although the disease declined in 1847, it came back in its full might in 1848 and 1849. The blight persisted because the Irish were dependent on this single crop, the potato, and they also lacked genetic varieties. They were constantly planting the same species that lacked resistance to *Phytophthora infestans,* allowing the fungus to thrive. The crisis persisted, and although there are no exact numbers of people who succumbed to the famine, estimates range between 775,000 and one million people. Most people died not of famine but of diseases such as typhus and cholera. Because of the lack of food, people ate raw turnips, seaweed, wild mustard, and fire nettle, as well as the rotting carcasses of domestic animals such as horses, dogs, and cattle that died due to illness. The people also died of hunger edema (famine dropsy) and scurvy, as they lacked Vitamin C in their diet, as well as various infections contracted in overcrowded workhouses and soup kitchens.

Those who were sufficiently strong and had some savings started running away from Ireland. In the autumn of 1846, many cottiers left, and in January of 1847, they were followed by small farmers. The movement of Irish people looked more like a mass exodus than emigration. They walked from the western parts of the island to Dublin, where they would embark for the shores of England. By June 1847, more than 300,000 Irishmen landed in Liverpool, straining the relief supplies of the city. The poorest of them all remained in England, but those who could afford to travel opted for North America. Most of them landed in the United States. There were not enough ships to transport all the people who wanted to sail, and many coal barges and cattle ships started receiving passengers. However, these ships were not suited for long human transport and soon turned into coffin ships. One-sixth of all the people who sailed for Canada in 1847 died during the voyage or immediately upon arrival.

During a single decade, from 1845 until 1855, more than 2.1 million men, women, and children escaped Ireland. Because there was no state census system implemented yet, the estimations are that Ireland lost one-quarter of its people to immigration during that period. The loss of population was accompanied by a drastic drop in small farm estates. The cottier class almost disappeared and was replaced by the modern agricultural pattern of Ireland—a family farm. In the western area of the island, poverty persisted longest, and so did the cottiers. The subdivision of the land by tenants ended, and the whole society of Ireland was experiencing a change. Late marriage became more common, and fewer children were being born. Larger farms grew in numbers, and the large landowners survived the famine. But the population decline led to lower rents, and 10 percent of the landowners filed for bankruptcy in the immediate post-famine period. Land properties were being sold, broken into smaller units, and bought by the landlords who managed to prosper even during the hardship. Because of this, the landlords were being blamed for the famine, together with the British government. This resentment towards the rich landowners grew deep in the people of Ireland, who now harbored a sentiment towards drastic actions. On January 13, 1847, The Irish Confederation was founded by William Smith O'Brien and John Mitchel. They secured the election of two MPs to the British Parliament and publicly supported the use of violence against the British.

O'Brien traveled to France to learn from the revolutionaries who had managed to overthrow the monarchy and install a republic in 1848. He came back home inspired and set up a war directory to plan and launch unrest. The first unrest occurred on July 29, 1848, and is colloquially remembered as the "Battle of Widow McCormack's Cabbage Patch." The shooting between the rebels and police lasted for several hours. It was the police who fired first, and O'Brien's people complained the shooting was unjustified, as they never provoked the police. O'Brien and Mitchel were arrested, and together they were condemned under the Treason Felony Act and transported to Tasmania, a British penal colony. After this, the Young Ireland movement collapsed, and the Irish Confederation merged with the Repeal Association, abandoning its violent past. But the tragedy of the Great Famine lingered, and it seared the survivors with horrible memories. The people would yet resort to force, but for the next twenty years, their sentiment toward violent measures would lie dormant.

Chapter 8 – Fight for Independence

A photo portrait of Charles Stewart Parnell

The Great Famine diminished the population of Ireland, but those who survived and chose to stay had reinforced spirits. Those layers of society that still needed to fight for their landowning and liberty rights stirred again, and new efforts to secure self-governance erupted. But Ireland was still divided, not only religiously but politically. While some groups sought to secure their rights by force, others chose a cooperative course, trying to bring back the Irish Parliament. Like so many times before, the force failed again, but the spirit was not crushed. Under the guidance of Charles Stewart Parnell (1846-1891), Ireland continued to work for its independence by constitutional means—peacefully but painstakingly slow. They achieved little. In the early 20th century, a new political party was founded, Sinn Féin, which called for an independent Irish Republic. Constitutional efforts registered some progress, and the beginning of the century was marked by the emergence of small, independent farmers.

Ireland was still not united, and many divisions—religious, political, and social—turned the country into a tension-filled island that was about to explode. But before violence could erupt into a civil war, World War I began. While Europe suffered violence on a cataclysmic scale, the unionists rushed to defend Great Britain. Some nationalists were intent to use the war that ravaged the whole world to strike at the ruling power in 1916, but the government managed to repress them. Nevertheless, they stirred the consciousness of their countrymen and awakened sympathy for a national republic. The Irish people remembered this sentiment when World War ended, and the republican rebels picked up their fight for independence once again. The result was another division of Ireland and the Irish people. The whole island was partitioned, and two constitutional monarchies were created, leaving many resentments on either side. The northern monarchy was tightly tied to the United Kingdom, while the southern one kept loose bonds with the previous government. After 700 years, the British finally gave up on Ireland, but when they left, society was still divided: geographically, politically, and religiously.

Home Rule Takes Shape and the Leadership of Parnell

The social, economic, and political power of the 19th century was concentrated in the hands of those who owned the land, just as it had always been in Ireland. A small number of landlords, only around 800, owned more than half the available land, but a variety of landowning arrangements existed in the second half of the century. Not all landlords were wealthy; their economic status depended greatly on various factors, such as the part of Ireland they lived in (the west was always significantly poorer), the amount of land they owned, the wages they paid their employees, and so on. The relationship between landowners and tenants was resentful, mainly because the tenants wanted more security in holding the land. The Irish Tenant League was founded in 1850, and it gathered tenants all over Ireland in a union that demanded lower rent from the landowners. In the parliamentary elections of 1852, the League won forty seats. However, it failed to bring forth legislative change and only spiraled downwards to its destruction a few years later.

The Fenian Brotherhood was founded in America in 1858, and it gathered emigrated Irish to counter the British government and advocate for the independence of Ireland. The same year, an Irish counterpart of the organization was founded in Ireland, named the Irish Republican Brotherhood. All members of these two organizations were known as the "Fenians," and they were not shy about using force to achieve their goals. They filled their ranks with the working class, and by 1866, they numbered thousands of laborers, artisans, clerks, farmers, and schoolteachers. They gathered both rural and urban Irishmen at home and abroad. The Fenians were almost purely Catholic organizations, but they advocated for an Irish republic that would guarantee equality for all. They also wanted a strict separation of church and state. But when the revolt was about to occur in 1866, the American branch of the Fenians failed to deliver promised weapons, and action was aborted. The uprising finally came the next year, but it was limited to a few local skirmishes that were quickly quelled. After yet another failed revolt, the leadership of the Fenians changed, and with it, the use of violence was downplayed. The organization concentrated its effort on inspiring people into activism.

Although the Fenians failed in their revolution, they did manage to inspire the British statesman William E. Gladstone (1809–98), who finally realized that the Irish question was of vast importance. He was the leader of the Liberal Party and a proud Anglican. In 1868, he became prime minister, serving in the office until 1874. Under his leadership, the government brought two major legislative changes which shaped the new Anglo-Irish relationship. The first one was the disestablishment of the Church of Ireland. The Irish Church Act of 1869 ended the privileges of the Church of Ireland, separating it from the state. This meant that the Protestant minority belonging to this church was no longer the main drive behind the state politics of Ireland. The disestablishment act also meant the end of the Protestant Ascendancy. The second piece of legislation was the Land Act of August 1, 1870, by which evicted tenants were compensated for their losses. This act was largely ineffective, but it represents the first time the British government paid attention to the rights of tenants.

In 1870, the nationalists of Ireland founded the Home Rule, a movement that called for the return of the Irish Parliament. Home Rule was led by Isaac Butt (1813–79), an Irish barrister who entered Parliament as a conservative MP. He was moved by the suffering his people experienced during the Great Famine, and he was inspired by the efforts of the Fenians. Butt was aware that the complete independence of Ireland was impossible at this moment, but a separate parliament was a more realistic option in his eyes. In the elections of 1874, Butt's Home Rule won more than half of the

Irish seats in the House of Commons. They spent the next five years pushing for a separate parliament, following all the procedures of the British government.

During the winter of 1878-79, the weather was unusually wet, threatening crop failure and another disaster like the Great Famine. Many landlords went bankrupt due to hard times. People all over Ireland faced starvation, bankruptcy, and eviction. Local Fenians held a meeting at Irishtown (Mayo County) to start a campaign that would avert the crisis. For support, the Fenians looked to a young but rising Irish politician, Charles Stewart Parnell (1846-91). Parnell worked to persuade Home Rule and their leader Isaac Butt to move from following the slow and passive parliamentary procedures to more active tactics, most notably refusal to cooperate with the House of Commons. Butt opposed the new tactics, but he died in 1879, and Parnell assumed the leading position within Home Rule. He joined forces with the leadership of the Fenians, Michael Davitt (1846-1906), and together they founded the Irish National Land League. Parnell was the president of the League, while Davitt was its chief organizer. Together they recruited members of all stripes, from moderates to radicals. Many bishops and Catholic clergy supported the League, and branch Leagues rose in the United States and Britain. The main goal of the League was the agrarian rights of the people; it organized resistance to the landlords, trying to prevent the eviction of tenants. Its main, long-term goal was to transform tenants into property owners. The so-called land war lasted from 1879 until 1882, and during it, many tenants were evicted. To fight this, they came up with a new tactic—the boycott. An embargo was put on the farms that evicted their tenants, and the economic and social contact of the landowners was completely cut off. The word boycott came from the name of a land agent from County Mayo, Captain Charles Boycott (d. 1897).

The League led their war against the landlords by putting out demands for the "Three Fs": fair rent, fair sale, and fixture of tenure. But their activism aroused passions, and naturally, violence broke out. The government sought to quell the violence, but its hands were tied against the National Land League because it was a legal body. The other difficulty was that the League had the strong support of Parliament. During the 1880s, the League assumed the powers of the local courts, and it provoked the government by encouraging rural people into violence. Finally, London gave a green light, and the arrests of the League leaders began. In February of 1881, Davitt was among the first to be arrested. But in August, Parliament passed a new land act by which the "Three Fs" were legalized. The government set up special courts in which tenants could apply for a fair rent ruling, and a system of shared ownership was introduced. But the Irish National League still wasn't satisfied, and it continued to agitate the people into unrest. The government responded by arresting all principal members of the League, including Parnell himself. But they only managed to anger this Irish politician, and he issued the "No Rent Manifesto" from his prison cell in Dublin's Kilmainham jail. In the manifesto, Parnell resumed his earlier calls for the nationals to organize a rent strike. However, most tenants and farmers were satisfied with the act the government had passed and didn't respond to Parnell's calls.

The League continued to operate and organize small, localized unrest. But by March of 1882, Parnell made an agreement, the so-called Kilmainham Treaty, with the government, promising to call off all disturbances in return for concessions to tenants. The government stopped arresting members of the League, and those who were already in jail were released. In 1883, Parliament passed the Arrears of Rent Act which, together with the Act of 1881, reduced the landowners' interests in holding onto their estates. Landlords started selling their properties to their tenants on favorable terms. In 1885, the government introduced a system by which the tenants received help to purchase the land. This made tenants satisfied, as they had achieved their final goal: the right to own their own land. There was no more need for the Irish National Land League, and it was soon replaced with a new organization, the Irish National League, founded on October 17, 1882.

The National League shifted the focus of its actions from agrarian rights to the Irish right to govern themselves. Davitt and Parnell believed that if they could eliminate the landlord class, that would be a start for removing the British government from the island. The activists of the League now worked on securing other Irish grievances, mainly the national parliament. Parliamentary elections of 1885 brought sweeping victory to Parnell and his partisans. The members who pledged to uphold Home Rule took eighty-five Irish seats in parliament, and with this number, they were able to balance out the two dominant British parties, the Liberals and the Conservatives. On April 8, 1886, the bill of Home Rule was put before the House of Commons, asking for the devolution of powers over domestic affairs to the Irish national Parliament. But the Conservative Party saw the bill as a step backward, towards the disunity of Great Britain, and as a betrayal. By June 8, 1886, the bill was voted out by the Conservatives and disaffected Liberals. Nevertheless, the attempt to introduce the Irish Parliament once again marked a new relationship between England and Ireland. A large part of the Liberal Party was devoted to Home Rule, and it allied with the nationalists in Ireland. This alliance even survived the divide within the Irish nationalists in 1891, when they split between Parnellite and anti-Parnellite factions.

The Nationalists and the Unionists

An ex-Fenian journalist, Arthur Griffith (1871–1922), founded a new society in September of 1900, the so-called Sinn Féin. His society's official policy was that Ireland should be a separate monarchy that would share the monarch with Great Britain but have a separate government. In 1905, Griffith's society turned into a political party when he issued a policy in which he proclaimed the act of union in 1800 illegal. Sinn Féin can be translated into English as "We Ourselves" or "Ourselves Alone," and in 1906, a newspaper with the same name was launched. The members of the Irish Republican Brotherhood were attracted by the policy of the new political party, and they joined in great numbers. But the new members radicalized the policy of the party, moving it from advocacy of a separate parliament to demanding complete independence. In 1908, Sinn Féin tested the political waters by running for Parliament in the elections. The party lost by two votes, but such a near victory demonstrated that, with a little bit more work, they would win a wide popular appeal.

Sinn Féin started spreading its influence and winning local elections. It attracted the attention of Constance Countess Markievicz (or Markiewicz, 1868-1927), who launched the Fianna Éireann movement in 1909, which advocated the Irish Republic. Soon, her efforts were joined by actress Maud Gonne, who founded a feminist movement, Inghinidhe na hÉireann (Daughters of Ireland). Together, they attracted the people who felt shunned by male republican groups, namely women and youth. But while these groups were all peaceful, the Irish Republican Brotherhood continued advocating for an Irish republic through force. They, too, suffered internal division, just like Parnell's League, but they managed to rebuild a core of militants and started drawing many recruits. Some of their prominent members were Patrick Pearse, the scholar and poet; Thomas MacDonagh, a professor at Dublin's University; and Seán MacBride, the ex-husband of feminist leader Maud Gonne.

Both Sinn Féin and the Irish Republican Brotherhood (IRB) opposed the policies of the Irish Parliamentary Party, which only sought to achieve a separate parliament. But at the turn of the 20th century, a new social layer emerged, one that had no interest in the political struggle—the working class. They had existed since the foundation of the first industries in Ireland, but finally, they represented most of the population. They shifted the focus of social life from the countryside to the cities. The matters of the landowners and tenants were part of the Irish past, and the working class now needed to fight for their rights. In so many towns across Ireland, laborers lived in poverty; they were badly fed and had low wages. In 1913, the IRB's newspaper, *Irish Freedom*, reported that over one-third of Dublin's population was underfed. To give a voice to their grievances, the laborers founded the Irish Transport and General Workers' Union (ITGWU) in 1908. The leader was James Larkin (1876-1947), and he organized Belfast dockworkers into a disciplined, nonsectarian force able to mount strikes against large companies. But Larkin was uninterested in the national interests of Ireland; he only cared about the workers' rights. He used all means necessary to achieve his goals, including violence. But the Belfast strike collapsed because, despite Larkin's effort to unite the workers, they were deeply divided by religion. The hatred between Protestants and Catholics was deeply rooted in Ireland, and the unity of the two religious factions once again proved impossible to sustain.

When the Liberals, under the leadership of Herbert Asquith (1852-1928), achieved a victory in 1910, a new prospect of sectarian violence emerged. Liberals and Conservatives were represented and won equal votes, and a liberal government could be formed only with the support of the Irish Parliamentary Party. The new government introduced a third Home Rule bill in 1912, calling for the foundation of a bicameral Irish Parliament in Dublin, with powers to legislate all domestic affairs. The British government would still have control over the police, but only for six years. They would also be responsible for the defense of Ireland, foreign policy, religious questions, and customs duties. In turn, the Parliament in London would have to admit forty-two Irish PMs, down from the previous 103. This bill seemed likely to pass, and the Unionists sought to gain special status for Ulster, where they represented the majority. Earlier, in 1905, they had founded the Ulster Unionist Party as an answer to Home Rule. In June of 1912, amendments were added to the bill to exclude the provinces of Armagh, Antrim, Down, and Londonderry. Irish Unionists approved of this change in the bill, but the amendments failed in the House of Commons.

Negotiations continued but were more difficult because, in Ulster, the atmosphere was becoming restless. On September 28, the Unionists organized an event in which three-quarters of Ulster citizens signed a pledge to oppose Home Rule. They also pledged that if the Home Rule government were to be elected, they would refuse its recognition. In January of 1913, the Unionists created the Ulster Volunteer Force to put muscle behind their words. The members of the Orange Order joined in masses, and soon the force numbered over 10,000 well-trained men, ready to resist. By April of 1914, the Ulster Volunteer Force illegally imported thousands of rifles and millions of rounds of ammunition to arm themselves. They were ready to set up an alternative regime if the need occurred under the leadership of Sir Edward Carson (1854–1935), the head of the Ulster Unionist Party.

In response to the Ulster Volunteer Force, the nationalists organized their own force, the Irish (National) Volunteers, on November 25, 1913. It took them only a few months to enroll up to 75,000 members. They had double the members of the Ulster counterpart, but they lacked weapons and training. At the same time, the labor strike broke out and only added to the already existing tensions in Ireland. In August 1913, William Martin Murphy (1844–1919), head of the Employer's Federation, dismissed around forty members of the ITGWU. He also planned to lock out the workers who refused to pledge against joining the union. In August and September, the tram workers went on strike, preventing the workers from reaching factories, storehouses, and dockyards. The largest and the most intense industrial battle in

Ireland had started, and it included riots, rallies, arrests and imprisonment—and even deaths. A citizen's army was created to protect the workers on strike, and it remained in use until the turmoil slowed down in January of 1914.

Women joined to support their male counterparts, and they founded the Irish Women Workers' Union (IWWU), a group within the ITGWU. This group was founded by James Larkin's sister, Delia Larkin (1878-1949). Although they started by opening soup kitchens for the strikers, they soon added their own voices to the fight. They also joined the British and American women in their fight for the right to vote. Isabella Tod (1836–96), a journalist from Belfast, formed the first society to promote women's suffrage as early as 1871. Delia Larkin represented working women within society, contrasting similar movements in Britain and the US, which were led by middle and upper-class women. In 1912, Hannah Sheehy Skeffington (1877-1946) founded the Irish Women's Suffrage League, an organization responsible for many large rallies of women. Skeffington was even arrested for destructive actions she undertook during one such rally organized in June of 1912. The women of Ireland and their suffrage movements supported Irish independence and backed up the Sinn Féin.

The third Home Rule bill was introduced three times to Parliament by the summer of 1914. On May 25, the House of Commons passed the bill, but the House of Lords and the Ulster Unionist Party actively sought to exclude Ulster from the Home Rule provisions. Prime Minister Asquith sought a compromise and allowed the "temporary" exclusion of Ulster and its six counties for an indeterminate period. But the House of Lords defeated the bill for the third time. The Parliament Act of 1911 states that a veto by the House of Lords will be overridden if a bill passed by the House of Commons is denied in three sessions over two years. The Home Rule bill was sent for royal assent.

In the meantime, while waiting for royal approval, Ireland bristled with tension. The spring and summer of 1914 brought these tensions to a culmination point, and both sides of the conflict were readying themselves for war. When rumors started that the British army stationed in County Kildare would be used to push the public to accept the Home Rule, fifty-seven out of seventy officers submitted their resignation. Germany, on the other hand, sent a ship filled with armaments to help the Irish Volunteers. The British army tried to prevent the ship from landing but failed, and the Volunteers received guns. By August, more guns arrived, and the competition between the nationalists and unionists was so tense that everyone thought a civil war was imminent.

The Rebellion during the World War

King George V (r. 1910-1935) signed the Government of Ireland Act on September 18, 1914. To celebrate the event, the Irish nationalists lit bonfires all over the country's hilltops and mountains. But their joy was cut short when the House of Commons voted at the same time to suspend the act for one year because a European war demanded their immediate attention. It was expected that the war would be short and easily won and that Parliament would soon do its regular business. However, the war proved to be much longer, and it turned from a European to a World War. On August 4, 1914, Britain declared war on Germany in protest of the German army's invasion into Belgium. All of Great Britain had to prepare for a war that demanded the urgent attention of Parliament and the public. The threat of this war was far greater than what was brewing in Ireland. Both nationalists and unionists answered the call to join the army of Great Britain. The Irish Volunteers offered themselves for home defense, but by September, they all received the call to enlist for service. The Irish Volunteers were soon known as the National Volunteers, but they never forgot their main goal—the self-rule of Ireland. In fact, the Volunteers hoped that they could use this war to demonstrate the fitness of the nationalists for self-government and earn the trust of their enemies, the unionists.

The unionists joined the war effort once they secured the suspension of the Home Rule. The officers of the Ulster Volunteer Force set up a 36th Ulster Division. In general, around 200,000 men, both Catholics and Protestants, joined the British army. Among them were many expatriates in Britain and the US. United by a common cause, the Irish men shared the suffering of the Great War. In the Battle of the Somme, on July 1, 1916, the Ulster Division was torn to pieces, all of them massacred by German machine guns.

War brought unexpected economic disruption to Ireland. With so many men leaving for war, the unemployment numbers dropped, and those who stayed enjoyed considerable prosperity. Farmers fared the best since they produced the food to feed the army, and the demand for their goods only increased. The foreign competition of the British market was cut off, and domestic production rose. Prices were on the rise; they even doubled between 1914 and 1918, and producers were getting rich. The inflation of prices led to easier access to agricultural credit. The small farmers were now able to buy agricultural machinery, and they joined cooperatives in large numbers.

A small number of dedicated republicans saw the war as an excuse to launch an armed resistance. They reasoned that if Britain was in distress, Ireland could succeed. The war distracted many of the British forces and the British government, allowing the republicans to strike a decisive blow. In September of 1914, the council of the Irish Republican Brotherhood met and convinced the provincial committee of the Irish Volunteers to abandon their leadership and join the insurrection. The American Clan na Gael was eager to finance the uprising. Roger Casement (1864–1916), a British consul and an Irish nationalist, traveled to Germany to secure their help in the Irish insurrection. The plan was to take the

Irish among the British prisoners of war and organize them into a brigade that would be hauled to Ireland together with the shipment of weapons.

But the planners of the insurrection forgot to take one factor into account: they didn't secure public support. The general public was against the rebellion because the tension of the Great War occupied them. The massive recruitment of people into the war effort resulted in IRB losing its members, and the Sinn Féin and the Gaelic League fell into inactivity when the war started. The republican activists were a minority, driven by fanaticism and pent-up frustration. The public was largely hostile towards them. In the best case, it was indifferent, but nobody in Ireland openly supported them. Another fact the republicans failed to consider was that even though the government was distracted, the war gave it access to a massive army that could be used to quell any resistance. And the government was aware of the brewing conspiracy in Ireland. The initial response of the government was to shut down several republican organizations and cancel their journals, which they used for recruitment. The officials at Dublin Castle did nothing else to stop the upcoming revolt because they thought there was no need for more action. Home Rule was expected, and the administration set up before the war functioned only as a temporary solution. When the German shipment of arms was sunk in April of 1916, the government relaxed even more and planned to spend the Easter holiday in a peaceful atmosphere.

The conspirators were disheartened, but it was their very demoralization that drove them to launch an attack earlier than planned. They had spent time and resources plotting, and it was too late to go back. The Military Council of the IRB thought that if the uprising failed, at least it would produce several martyrs and awaken the patriotic spirit in the people who still dreamed of the Irish Republic. Creating martyrs was now their goal, and with that in mind, they chose not to attack key governmental positions such as

Dublin Castle or Trinity College. Instead, they gathered in the city center where they could attract maximum attention by seizing property and taking human lives if necessary.

The uprising began on Easter Monday morning, on April 24, and is remembered in history as the Easter Rising. Residents of Dublin were awakened by machine-gun fire. The Irish Volunteers and the Irish Citizens' armies, numbering 1,600 men, set up their headquarters in the General Post Office building at the very center of the shopping district. Patrick Pearse, a teacher and one of the leaders of the uprising, read the "Proclamation of the Irish Republic" from the stairs of the Post Office. Small forces seized other offices, buildings, parks, bridges, and factories, intending to create defense points in them. Young women, members of the radical republican group Cumann na mBan, acted as messengers and couriers for the rebels. Constance Markievicz, the founder of this women's organization, served as second in command at the rebel's garrison at St. Stephen's Green, a public park in the city center of Dublin.

The uprising lasted for six days, and the government responded immediately with martial law and the shipment of defensive troops from Britain. Six days of death and devastation ensued, as heavy shelling reduced the rebels' strongholds one by one. The last stronghold to fall was at Boland's Mill, where the commander in chief, Patrick Pearse, surrendered on April 29. The rebels suffered only sixty-four casualties, while the British army had 132. But the civilians fared the worst, with over 318 killed and 2,217 wounded. Also, they had to endure the widespread looting and destruction of their property. The public responded with anger, and the citizens threw tomatoes at the defeated rebels as they were led to execution. Up to fifteen ringleaders, including Pearse, were quickly executed by a firing squad. Martial law gave the British army the right to act without limited power, and an insurrection such as this in a time of war meant betrayal. However, the army went too far by arresting several thousand Irish people who had no connection to the rebellion just because of their political convictions. Ironically, the government's response achieved what the rebels had failed to do, and the public opinion turned against them. All the efforts to provoke Anglo-Irish reconciliation through the Home Rule campaign and the common cause of the Great War disappeared, and hostility towards the government was reignited in the Irish.

Prime Minister Asquith was aware the government went too far, and he pulled back the army, stopping further executions and incarcerations. He released those who were wrongfully arrested and relaxed martial law. But it was too late—the people felt a surge of nationalism in them, no matter their political opinions. The revolution remained a constant threat, and the new government, under the leadership of liberal David Lloyd George (1863–1945), hurried to secure the Home Rule settlement with the exclusion of six counties of Ulster only for the duration of the war. The unionists disapproved of this settlement, and the agreement fell apart. The result was the end of the Irish Parliamentary Party, as its leaders went separate ways in pursuing their goals. Although the government gave up its efforts to resolve the question of Ireland while the war continued, the republicans didn't launch another rebellion. They realized it would fail again and again and that the better tactic was to work on a campaign that would change the public opinion and gain their support.

Free State of Ireland

At the end of the war, the Sinn Féin party activated again and was working hard to recruit as many people as possible to the republican cause. The party chose not to resort to arms to push their agenda but to use the elections to win the majority and push for the republican appeal. In October of 1917, Eamon de Valera was elected president of Sinn Féin, while Arthur Griffith was his vice president. At the same time, the party announced its main goal was to have Ireland recognized as an independent republic. While

Sinn Féin recruited people and worked on its political plans, the IRB went through reconstruction. All its military members were executed after the Easter Rebellion, but a new leader emerged—Michael Collins (1890-1922), a former London clerk. Collins also played a crucial role in the Irish Volunteers, which was reorganized in October 1917. The Volunteers remained a national defense, ready to rise if called. They paraded, drilled, and stirred small, local insurrections while taking care never to attack soldiers or police. The prospect of another rebellion arose when Prime Minister Lloyd George, under the renewed German threat, rushed to pass the law of conscription in Ireland. The Home Rule MPs protested and withdrew from Parliament, and Sinn Féin organized demonstrations. On April 21, thousands of people signed a "solemn council pledge" to oppose the conscription, and the next day the workers went on strike. By May, the Sinn Féin leaders were arrested and accused of plotting with Germany. But the public opinion was acknowledged, and instead of conscription, a quota scheme for voluntary enlistment was introduced. The issue lost its weight when, on November 11, the armistice was signed in France.

Sinn Féin's absolute resistance to the conscription brought popularity to the party. Its presence spread to places where it had no representation before. At the general elections of 1918, Sinn Féin won a sweeping victory and claimed 73 out of 106 seats. The Home Rule constitutional nationalists were utterly destroyed. Sinn Féin representatives were mostly young Catholics from the middle classes, and they even included several women among them, such as Constance Markievicz. The support for this party was so widespread that, in the elections of 1920, they took 172 seats out of 206 county and city council posts. But Sinn Féin's members pledged not to take parliamentary seats at Westminster; instead, the party's parliament met at the Mansion House in Dublin, where they proclaimed themselves the first Dáil Éireann—the Parliament of Ireland—and declared independence from Britain. The first acting president of

Dáil Éireann was Cathal Brugha (1874–1922), but he was replaced quickly by Eamon de Valera, who started dominating political life in Ireland. The first objective of the independent parliament was to secure foreign support, and de Valera went on a tour of the United States for eighteen months. He referred to himself as the president of the Irish Republic, and he managed to raise millions of US dollars in support of Irish independence. His cause was eagerly accepted in the US because its new president, Woodrow Wilson (1856–1923), popularized the premise that free peoples should have the right to govern themselves.

But Michael Collins of the IRB had equally popular status as de Valera. He became minister of finance and the president of the Supreme Council of IRB in 1919. He was a potential enemy of de Valera, and this rivalry only highlighted the disunion of authority in Ireland. The Dáil used 1919 and 1920 to set up new governmental institutions, and it put in place ministers mirroring those of the official government. Countess Markievicz became the first woman in office in Western Europe when she was appointed minister of labor.

The Protestants went back to the hostilities they had harbored towards the Irish nationalists during the pre-war period. However, the unionists' opinions changed, and they now advocated for the partition of the country. They were afraid that if Ireland gained its independence, they would become a minority ruled by Dublin. Their religious, economic, and social interests would never be equally represented. But many Protestants in the south of the island were accustomed to being a minority. They represented only one-tenth of the population there, and they worked on reconciliation with the Catholics. They wanted to live in a united, self-governed Ireland that would have complete freedom in domestic affairs but would leave foreign affairs to London. In the north, the Ulster Volunteer Force was revived in 1920, determined to defend their

Protestant-dominated territory. The Catholic minority among them protested but was unable to do anything.

In addition to the sectarian division of the country, the labor forces were on strike again. The post-war period brought rising unemployment and economic hardship. By 1920, ITGWU had more than 100,000 members, including both skilled and unskilled workers, and strike activities spread all over the country. In the countryside, the situation was similar. The agricultural prices began to fall because the market had opened again. By late 1920, the unemployment rate was higher than in the pre-war era, and wages fell. The scattered local councils of workers started taking over the management of their industries. But outside of Ulster, labor strikes were localized and small and were unable to generate significant threat. The republicans started building ties with the Irish Labor Party founded in 1912, linking the worker's grievances to the national cause. In mid-April of 1920, a general worker shutdown was organized in solidarity with the republicans, who went on hunger strikes. All this unrest in the north caused yet another sectarian divide. The Ulster Unionists Labor Association (founded in 1918) expelled Catholic workers from factories and shipyards. From July to September, Belfast was the site of many riots, which led to more than thirty deaths.

Resolved to end the military buildups in Ireland caused by the nationalists and the unionists, the government introduced a new bill to Parliament calling for the creation of two separate parliaments in Ireland: one in Dublin and the other in Belfast. The Ulster Unionist Council accepted this compromise, and on December 23, 1912, the bill was passed into law as the Government of Ireland Act. The executive authority was still in the hands of the Crown, and its executer would be lord-lieutenant, as before. A Council of Ireland would coordinate the issues which were of concern to both parliaments. The members of the council would be voted in by both parliaments, and the hopes were that this council would, in fifty years, evolve into a single Parliament of Ireland. Both northern and southern Ireland would continue to send MPs to Westminster.

But between February and December of 1920, the months in which all of Ireland waited for the bill to pass or be declined, the country was in chaos. The government continued to negotiate with both nationalists and unionists as if the bill was still open to discussion. This created tension as each party continued to push for its own agenda. The administration at Dublin castle continued to operate as if Home Rule would become the dominant regime. The Dáil carried out its business as a fully functioning government. Their allies, the Irish Volunteers, conducted a series of arsons, raids, intimidations, and ostracization operations to intimidate the population to accept the Dáil as the only solution to government. The Irish Volunteers became the Irish Republican Army (IRA), the official army of the republic that strived to implement a nationwide strategy to import arms. On September 7, the IRA openly attacked the British army at Fermoy, County Cork, launching the war for independence. Several days later, the British administration declared Dáil Éireann an illegal assembly. The British government started a campaign of harsh repressions, but it only managed to push the republicans closely together as they ran to avoid arrests. They continued to fight guerilla battles in which they would strike hard suddenly and disappear quickly. But the British authorities were ready to answer the challenge, and their armed forces compelled republicans to switch their tactics to small-scaled attacks.

Since de Valera was absent for much of the time, Collins took leadership of the armed forces of the resistance. The IRB included in its membership some of the prominent IRA leaders, which allowed him to earn legendary status for his efforts to organize guerilla and espionage tactics against the British government. He was on the British list of most wanted men. The British army and the Royal Irish Constabulary (RIC) organized brutal and horrific repressions on the IRA and the general populace of Ireland. They were all veterans of World War I and were ruthless in the war against the Irish insurrections. Raids and ambushes were common occurrences across the island, and local authorities were often forced to choose a side. The war culminated on November 21, 1920, when the IRA executed fourteen people suspected of espionage for the British government. The British government's regiment, known as the "Black and Tans" because of the colors of their uniform, opened fire during a football game in Dublin, killing twelve spectators. Many more died in the ensuing stampede, and the day is remembered in the history of Ireland as "Bloody Sunday." In reprisal, the IRA killed eighteen-men patrols of the auxiliary forces. In Ulster, Catholics lived in perpetual fear of Protestant police officers known as the "B Specials," a division belonging to the Ulster Special Constabulary. Martial law was imposed in December 1920, but the police, IRA, and the military continued their war. They also started intruding into the lives of civilians, and no one felt safe anymore. The Irish War of Independence caused anger among the public of Ireland, Britain, and the US. Many war protests were organized, and a group called Peace Council was founded to work closely with the British politicians to stop the violence. The hostilities were suspended on July 9, 1921, because of the military stalemate and the constant war protests. Representatives of the IRA and the British army finally signed a truce.

The Government of Ireland Act from 1920 mandated parliamentary elections in northern and southern Ireland amidst the unrest. By the act, the counties of Antrim, Armagh, Down, Fermanagh, Londonderry, and Tyrone, as well as the boroughs of Belfast and Londonderry, defined Northern Ireland. The elections were held on May 21, 1921, and the unionists won. The north proved to be a one-party unionist state. The Northern Ireland House of Commons met on June 7, and Prime Minister James Craig (1871–1940) was appointed to the cabinet. In Southern

Ireland, Sinn Féin ran unopposed and won 120 out of 124 seats. But the Sinn Féin members boycotted the state opening of the southern parliament because they were supporters of the Dáil, which was proclaimed illegal. The result was the suspension of Parliament. The Government of Ireland Act predicted such an outcome and stipulated that if the parliament in the south didn't meet until July 12, the country would become the Crown's colony and martial law put in place. The Sinn Féin MPs elected to the southern Parliament met in the Mansion House with the four non-Sinn Féiners, and together they formed the second Dáil Éireann. They chose de Valera as their president. The killing had stopped by now, and the Dáil oversaw the rebuilding of the governmental institutions.

Prime Minister Lloyd George didn't want colonial rule under martial law in Ireland, and he announced that he was open to listening to all options for the political settlement in Ireland. He met with de Valera on July 14, and two months later, they organized a conference in London which was to gather the representatives of Britain and Ireland to discuss the solution. But the delegates of Northern Ireland decline the invitation. The Irish negotiators were led by Arthur Griffith and Michael Collins, and they managed to win considerable concessions to their government. The Dáil now officially had power over taxation, tariffs, and national and civil defense. But the Irish naval bases were to remain in Britain's hands. The draft treaty was signed in London on December 6, 1921, and the result was the creation of Saorstát Éireann—the Irish Free State. It wasn't a republic but a constitutional monarchy with a two-house parliament with power over independent domestic and foreign affairs. The British monarch still had executive powers, and he was represented in Dublin by a governor-general. All the members of the parliament were to take an oath of allegiance both to the monarch and to the Free State.

But de Valera and several ministers objected to swearing an oath of loyalty to Great Britain, even if it was through a symbolic oath to the king. Ten days of vigorous debates followed, and the Anglo-Irish Treaty was finally passed on January 7, 1922. But the voting was narrow—sixty-four to fifty-seven—and the treaty needed to be ratified by the Irish Parliament elected earlier, as the British government still refused to acknowledge the Dáil Éireann. The Parliament of Southern Ireland finally met on January 14, approved the treaty, and elected a provisional government that would draft a constitution. Michael Collins was elected chairman of the provisional government, and he received the keys of Dublin Castle from the last lord-lieutenant of Ireland, Edward Fitzalan-Howard, on January 16. The symbolic transfer of power served to make it real in the minds of people that political change had finally happened.

An independent republic for all of Ireland never emerged, but it also wasn't an island-wide constitutional rule under Great Britain. The compromised solution of the two parliaments, one in the north and the other one in the south, was the best that could be expected in the turbulent politics of Ireland. But precisely because it was a compromise, many were left disappointed. There was no chance of reaching a settlement that would satisfy all political parties, religious groups, or worker labor unions. Ireland was profoundly divided, and the people identified with the injustices that were imposed on them. The creation of two Irelands didn't manage to heal all the wounds, and a turbulent political and public life continued. The call to arms that all of Ireland heard at one period of time, during the 700 years of struggle for political supremacy, can be heard even today.

Chapter 9 – The Making of Modern Ireland

A photo portrait of Eamon de Valera

The compromise that was the Anglo-Irish Treaty was designed to give all political parties a little bit of what they wanted, but not everything they fought for. In the north, the Protestants were the majority in their six counties, and their economy was largely dependent on industry. The south was a stark contrast to the north. Here, the Catholics were a majority, and they based their economy on agriculture and rural life. The northerners were very militant in defending their identity. The southerners gained so much more than what the Home Rule had promised them. They became a dominion within the British Empire, but a free state able to govern itself. But this wasn't enough for the republicans, who sought to sever all ties Ireland had with Great Britain. They launched yet another civil war but ultimately failed to secure independence.

The Irish Free State finally settled down and recognized the two Irelands, even though it kept its rhetoric against it. The republicans who had lost the civil war changed their tactics and entered politics to secure the existence of their nation. Eamon de Valera founded a new political party, Fianna Fáil, which stayed in power between the 1930s and 1960s. The constitution they promulgated achieved governance unfettered by its links with England. But this was not the end of the struggles. De Valera's party cherished traditional and conservative views on Ireland's Catholic heritage, promoting rural life as a direction they should continue to follow. However, with the quick industrialization of the world and the ensuing economy, backward-oriented Ireland couldn't keep up. Ireland was economically stagnant, and it started losing people again due to emigration.

During World War II, Ireland remained neutral, and the people of the south watched their northern counterparts join the fight and enjoy victory on the side of the Allies. The post-war years brought prosperity to Northern Ireland, but the south managed to finally make its dream come true: the emergence of the Republic of Ireland. But the new status of the republic didn't mean much to the people who continued to drown in poverty as the state struggled to pull itself out from old economic troubles. The new administration that took over during the 1960s finally launched more progressive politics that moved the country forward. A modern consumer society started to take hold of the whole island, and it started to weaken the Catholic Church's grasp on the life of the Irish people. The whole island prospered, except the small Catholic minority in the north, deeply set in their old ways. Ultimately, they were confined to a ghetto, and the Protestant unionists were determined to keep them there. But the discord between the two factions only grew over time, and during the 1960s, it finally exploded.

Turmoils Continue

The partition of Ireland suited most of the people. The Protestant unionists remained tied to the British Empire but had the freedom to control those ties. The south was finally able to govern itself, and the Catholics there thought Northern Ireland wouldn't be able to sustain itself and would soon ask to join their Free State. The only completely unsatisfied party was a group of Catholic citizens in the north, the minority which was now trapped among the Protestants. They were nationalists and republicans, and their ultimate goal was the Republic of Ireland that would include all thirty-two counties of the island. The British government wanted to separate the north by giving the unionists control over the nine counties of Ulster. But the unionists insisted that the number be reduced to six, as they were determined to include only the counties in which the Protestants were the majority. That way, they could control the Catholics and keep them a minority. Northern Ireland unionists elected their Parliament, and by the time the Anglo-Irish Treaty was adopted, they had a fully operational government. The treaty was intended for all of Ireland, but the north was given an option to choose if it wants to be included in the Free State or opt-out. The unionists chose the latter on December 7, 1922.

The Northern Irish Parliament consisted of a sovereign, a House of Commons, and a Senate. The Senate had modest power to amend legislation, and the power to pass the laws on major domestic issues was in the hands of the House of Commons. But the Northern Irish Parliament didn't have the power to meddle in foreign affairs, imperial matters, and military decisions. It couldn't make any laws that would promote religious discrimination, and it could not change any laws passed by the existing statute of the United Kingdom. The governor of Northern Ireland had the power to summon and dissolve Parliament and to give or withhold the royal assent to all the bills. Northern Ireland had to send thirteen MPs to the UK Parliament in London.

The new government of Northern Ireland was organized in such a way as to promote Protestant dominion. The Ulster Unionist Party (UUP) was the political instrument of control. The party leader, Sir Edward Carson, thought of the partition as a defeat for the unionist, who wanted the entirety of Ireland to stay closely related to Britain. He even refused to accept the office of prime minister. The leadership of Northern Ireland passed to Sir James Craig (1871–1940), Viscount Craigavon. The first years of the existence of Northern Ireland were very turbulent. Riots and sectarian strife were dominant in all its parts, and Londonderry and Belfast suffered the most. In 1922, around 232 lives were lost, including those of the unionist MPs. But the Catholics lost the most, as they were often attacked by the B-Specials. Their army, the IRA, was proclaimed illegal on May 23, 1922, and it consisted of very small numbers in the north.

Political life in Northern Ireland was completely controlled by the Protestants. The government was partially relying on the British army to keep order, but it also established a regular police force in May 1922, the Royal Ulster Constabulary (RUC), the successor of the Royal Irish Constabulary. Sectarian fraternities such as the Orange Order were very much alive, and the government relied on these Protestant loyalists to mobilize the people in their support. The Catholics made the existence of the Protestant government easy by refusing to participate in state institutions. One-third of the police force was a quota for the Catholics, but it remained unfilled. The Nationalist Party, organized out of the remnants of the old Irish Parliamentary Party in Ulster, joined forces with the Sinn Féin and entered the parliamentary elections of 1921. But the overall atmosphere of the elections was filled with violence and intimidation. The results were the unionists taking thirty-nine out of fifty-two seats of the House of Commons. The rest were divided between the Nationalists, the Irish Labor Party, and the Independents. But the Nationalists, who believed that the government always worked against them, decided to boycott the parliamentary sessions until 1925. This made it much easier for the unionists to redraw the constituencies in such a way as to gain full control of Parliament. The Catholics, usually members of the Sinn Féin that were members of the county council and other local bodies of government, refused to recognize the legitimacy of Northern Ireland. In 1922, the government moved to expel such individuals and suspend their membership within the governmental bodies.

With the creation of Northern Ireland, a new educational system was put in place. It was completely controlled and financed by the government, and religious teachings were purely voluntary. The Protestants agreed with this system, but the Catholics didn't want to allow religion to fall into a second plan in their children's education, and they operated their own schools, which were not entirely financed by the government but had its support. Catholics were usually left alone, and they created their own insular world. They secretly hoped that the partition of Ireland was only temporary, and their hopes were lifted when, in 1922, the borders were not yet strictly decided. Article 12 of the Anglo-Irish Treaty called for the creation of a commission in which both Northern and Southern

Ireland would be represented, as well as the UK. Together, they were supposed to define the borders in accordance with the wishes of popular opinion and following natural political and geographic conditions. This article evoked fears among the unionists who thought that the territory they controlled would be reduced by the commission. The decision about the borders was prolonged once again when the British government fell in 1923. The unionists now had time to gather their strength and oppose the wishes of the minority Catholics, who expected Tyrone and Fermanagh to be reunited with Southern Ireland.

Civil War in the South, The Shaping of the Free State

The creation of the Free State of Ireland split the members of the Sinn Féin between those who supported the Anglo-Irish Treaty and those who did not. The main problem within the agreement was the oath of allegiance to a British monarch. Some members of the party thought that the acceptance of a constitutional monarchy would give Ireland enough self-governing power to continue its fight for complete independence. But their opponents wanted the immediate creation of a republic because so many of their countrymen had lost their lives fighting for its realization. De Valera was the leader of the anti-treaty advocates. He even resigned his role as the president of the Dáil after the treaty was ratified. The new president of the Dáil was Arthur Griffith, a pro-agreement leader. The Dáil continued to exist and to meet, but the provisional government, under the leadership of Michael Collins, was the one that drafted the constitution. Thus, Griffith and Collins, the main negotiators of the treaty, were de Valera's bitter opponents.

The provisional government didn't have control over the army, the police force, or the court system. The country was just taking its shape, and the constitution was being written, yet the divide within its political setup was threatening the collapse of the Free State before it took its final shape. Most people voted pro-agreement, but the IRA sided with de Valera. Michael Collins was careful to word the new constitution in such a way as to appeal to those who were against the agreement, but the British government would have none of it. The third Dáil Éireann elections were held on June 16, 1922, and the voters approved the pro-treaty position of Parliament. But the losing side chose violence to achieve its goals. The election led to further division within the IRA and the Dáil. The "Old IRA" was a term used to refer to veterans who now joined the Free State army and backed the pro-agreement government. The uncompromising republicans were the "New IRA" or the "Irregulars" and the "Executives." They denounced the treaty and the Dáil, saying that by accepting the agreement, they would betray the republic. Military and social anarchy seemed like a possibility at the time, and the tension between the various factions was palpable.

In April of 1922, the IRA Irregulars occupied the judicial center in Dublin, challenging the authority of the provisional government. They occupied the Four Courts buildings (Irish Supreme Court) and demanded the transfer of rule to themselves. The face-off between the two sides lasted for two months, and neither the IRA nor the government backed down. On June 22, the IRA Irregulars assassinated Field Marshal Henry Wilson, and the British government started pushing the Irish provisional government to take action. On June 28, the forces of the Free State army attacked the Four Courts building, and by June 30, they recaptured it. Dublin was torn by violence once again. Activists quickly organized themselves on either side, but the anti-treaty group managed to gather a broad republican front. Civil war broke throughout the country, and the fighting was brutal and ruthless. The government managed to secure Dublin within two weeks and arrest some of the anti-agreement leaders. By mid-summer, the government held all the major cities and towns, while the Irregular made Munster their base of operation, particularly the Counties of Kerry, Cork, and Tipperary.

It took the government only three months to defeat the republicans in those counties, but it wasn't a decisive defeat. The republicans switched their tactics to mainly operating in the countryside, launching quick attacks and planning assassinations. The republicans had to destabilize the country to fight it effectively, and they proclaimed the provisional government, police, army, and courts of the Free State illegal. They started shooting the members of the Dáil known as Teachta Dála (TD for short), judges, and police and military officials on sight. Even journalists weren't spared, as they were considered government conspirators. On August 22, 1922, Michael Collins was ambushed and assassinated at Béal na Bláth, County Cork. This was the hardest blow to the provisional government. Arthur Griffith had died ten days earlier, and the Dáil was forced to elect a new president as the head of the provisional government. On September 9, the appointment was given to William T. Cosgrave (1880–1965), a member of Sinn Féin and the Dublin City Council. The next year, in 1923, Cosgrave founded his own political party in support of the agreement, Cumann na nGaedheal.

After the assassination of Collins, the provisional government decided to strike back at the republicans, and on November 22, they executed seventy-seven arrested Irregulars, giving them no opportunity to defend themselves in court. Around 12,000 more were imprisoned. But while fighting the republicans, the government also faced the threats of other factions. The Farmers' Union had been discontent about the curtailment of land purchases during the immediate after-war period, but they were now angry at the rural laborers who attacked them because of the wage cuts. The Laborers attacked the Farmers' Union first in Meath, but the major confrontation occurred in Waterford, where it lasted from 1921 to 1923. Another menace came from the industrial laborers, whose numbers swelled when the army returned from the war. The strength of the ITGWU in politics was reflected when the Labor

Party won 21.4 percent of the votes cast in the elections of 1922, even more than the anti-agreement forces.

Both the republicans and the government were anti-labor, rural-based, conservative nationalists, and during the labor unrest, IRA members were used as riot breakers. Farmers won the unrest in Waterford in 1923 with the support of the Free State army. By then, the pro-agreement government had won the civil war against the republicans. When the leader of the republican militant unit, Liam Lynch, was shot on April 10, 1923, the Irregulars collapsed. On May 24, de Valera instructed his followers to put down their arms and surrender. The end of the civil war left the provisional government and its supporters to finally create the Irish Free State in their own image.

On October 25, 1922, the government approved the bill that defined the constitution of the twenty-six counties comprising the Irish Free State. By December, the bill was passed by the British Parliament. The constitutional monarchy took shape, with a three-tiered Parliament (Oireachtas) composed of the monarch and a two-body legislature. The first legislative body was the lower house, the Chamber of Deputies (Dáil Éireann), which was the chief legislative body. The second was the upper house, the Senate (Seanad Éireann). The Senate was a body of elders that advised the lower house, but it had no powers to pass legislation, only to delay it. The lower house elected the members of the Senate except for one-quarter of the members, who were nominated by the British government. The intention behind the upper house was to give voice to the Protestant minority who remained in Southern Ireland and whose participation in politics was deemed essential. After all, allowing the Protestants to join the political life in Southern Ireland gave credence to the Irish Free State's claim to rule the whole island.

The king had executive authority, and he was represented by a governor-general. His authority was represented in-state by a cabinet called the Executive Council. It was presided over by the President of the Executive Council. The legal system of the Irish Free State was organized in 1924, and it followed the model in Britain. It included the district and circuit courts, high court, court of criminal appeal, and supreme court. Unlike its northern counterpart, Southern Ireland had no British police and army presence. The national police force, the Civic Guard, was founded on August 8, 1923, and in 1925, the Dublin Metropolitan Police was incorporated into it. In 1928, the Free State pound was introduced as the currency replacing the British pound, and the symbols of sovereignty, the flag, and the seal were adopted at the same time.

The newly-adopted constitution mandated the election of the new parliament within a year of the document's approval. The elections were held in August 1923, and Cumann na nGaedheal won the largest number of seats, sixty-six compared to Sinn Féin's forty-four. But the members of Sinn Féin elected to Parliament still refused to acknowledge the legitimacy of the Free State, and they refused to attend parliamentary sessions for nearly a decade. The country was led by one party, Cumann na nGaedheal, which had control of the early nation-building. Through the rest of the 1920s and the 1930s, the new government worked to give the country an identity as a uniquely Irish state. This meant that the new nation had to distance itself from the United Kingdom as much as possible. Efforts to weaken the ties of the Irish government with London were launched, and in 1923, the Free State joined the League of Nations without consulting the British government. Of course, the British objected because, in their opinion, the Free State was a dominion within the UK and had no right to make such a decision alone. Unlike any other dominion in the UK, the Free State of Ireland continued to sign treaties and send its ambassadors to other nations. In 1927, the Irish government won the ability to advise the king whom to appoint as governor-general, and Britain officially lost the ability to influence Irish domestic affairs.

The partition of Ireland left the south heavily dependent on agriculture. More than half of its labor force worked on farms by the mid-1930s. The economy of the Free State suffered as it struggled to keep up with the modern, industrialized world. During the 1930s, the government pursued a low tax, low-spending policy, the economic trend it had followed since the Great Famine. Land was sold to small farmers, while the medium and large farmers consolidated what they already owned. State-aided programs for buying cattle and poultry were implemented, and a new institution for obtaining loans, the Agricultural Credit Corporation, was founded in 1927. Nevertheless, Irish agricultural production remained extremely low for the European standards of the time.

After years of turmoil, de Valera finally decided to reconcile with the government and return to the political life of Ireland. He abandoned the leadership of Sinn Féin and started a new party, Fianna Fáil (Soldiers of Destiny), in 1926. But his political direction was long set in stone, and the new party was given the subtitle "The Republican Party," leaving no doubt of de Valera's ultimate goals. However, he abandoned his previous violent methods of achieving a republic and sought now to do it through involvement in Parliament. In the elections of 1927, his party won forty-four seats, while the Cumann na nGaedheal won forty-seven. De Valera's popularity was on the rise since he had the financing of Irish-Americans; he also addressed some of the serious grievances of both farmers and workers, such as low wages, emigration, small farmers' demands, and unemployment. Through his parliamentary participation, de Valera proved himself as a democratic politician. In 1931, his party won its first elections and formed its own government. For the first time, the anti-agreement politicians were in control of the Free State's government.

De Valera became the President of the Executive Council and a minister of foreign affairs, and he used the power of his offices to change Anglo-Irish relations. He manipulated the system to undermine the treaty, not by abolishing the parliamentary forms but by transforming them. First, he dismantled the symbols and then the substance of the dominion status. In 1933, he abolished the oath of loyalty, and in 1936, he attempted to abolish the governor-generalship and completely sever ties with the Crown. However, he was forced to back down as the governmental system of Britain didn't recognize the removal of institutions through legislative fiat. But de Valera brought forth the External Relations Act, which reduced the involvement of the monarch in the Irish government. The king became only a diplomatic representative of Ireland to foreign countries.

The Irish Free State became a republic in all but name when de Valera introduced a new constitution in 1937. It got approved by the Dáil on June 14 and by the public in a referendum held on July 1, 1937. The new name of the country, declared so by the constitution, was Éire (Ireland). The new constitution called for the election of a prime minister (Taoiseach), who would be the head of state, and a national Parliament (Oireachtas). Parliament would be composed of the lower house and upper house just as before, but both would have their powers reduced. To consolidate his power, de Valera used IRA units to gather supporters all over the country. The opposition, Cumann na nGaedheal, remained dominant only in Dublin. By the 1940s, the Fianna Fáil had a firm grasp on the political life of Ireland and the support of most of its population. But the IRA became responsible for some of the unrest within the country and several assassinations. Aware they were losing control of the militarized organization, the government declared the IRA illegal on June 18, 1936.

But the threats to parliamentary rule didn't come from the IRA. They came from a right-wing parliamentary group organized in 1933, the fascist National Guard. An ideology that glorified the nation was very appealing to the Irishmen, who were proud of their newly won independence. The National Guard was founded in 1933, and its leader was Eoin O'Duffy (1891–1944), who marveled at European dictators Benito Mussolini and Adolf Hitler. The Guard claimed to uphold Christian and anti-communist values, and it advocated the creation of a corporate state in which the employee and the employer, supported by the government, would take over the management of the national industry. The Guard was prepared to use violence to achieve its goals. The organization was declared illegal in August 1933, and O'Duffy united the National Guard with Cumann na nGaedheal to create a new political party, the United Ireland Party (later known as Fine Gael). This party claimed that their founder was late Michael Collins and that their origins were in the pro-treaty Sinn Féin faction. They saw themselves as the protectors of the state institutions and the force that upheld law and order. A year of violent parliamentary activism followed, and Fine Gael and Fianna Fáil renounced O'Duffy's leadership. However, these parties continued to exist and work within the boundaries of the parliamentary system and became two dominant parties in Ireland.

During the 1930s, the landscape of rural Ireland remained unchanged. It was painting an idealistic picture of the family farm life of the old ages. The republican political parties cherished this way of life and promoted it as a tradition that would always thrive. But in reality, the people were poor, living in small one-story cottages, able to cover only the necessities. Most of the people delayed getting married because they were not able to support a family. The ideal country life promoted by de Valera and his associates was just an illusion, and the proof for it was the increase in emigration. Since the Great Famine, people were leaving Ireland in hopes of finding a better life on different soil. Most of them emigrated to the US, Canada, and Britain. The population of the island dropped below three million. All the policies the government came up with to keep people in the country had failed.

But while the rural life remained unchanged, the cities were developing and rushing towards modernization, even though that was not the main objective of the government. By 1940, the Irish cities were electrified. The cinema and radio first came to Dublin in 1921, but during the 1930s, they were spreading throughout the country thanks to Anglo-American cultural agents, rare people who came back from emigration. They also brought automobiles with them, and by 1940, they swarmed the streets of the cities and towns. In August 1936, Ireland set up its first national airline, Aer Lingus, and the government was its sole shareholder.

North Goes to War

Almost twenty years after the division of Ireland, Europe plunged into yet another war of world proportions. But this war that erupted in 1939 showed how deep this division in Ireland was. When the UK declared war on Germany on September 3, Northern Ireland gave its wholehearted support. The people were anxious to show off their loyalty to the Crown, and Prime Minister Craigavon requested conscription for Northern Ireland. But the newly-elected Prime Minister of England, Winston Churchill (1874-1963), declined, as he was aware such a step would only antagonize the nationalists and maybe even stir the old turmoils that ravaged Ireland just decades ago. Nevertheless, enlistment in the army suffered no shortages, and by late 1941, the Northern Irish totaled 23,000 of all the British armed forces. But the war brought new woes to an already poor country. The National Guard was manned by the B-Specials, and they rationed food and other resources. Londonderry became an important naval base, but all over the country, airfields were being built, and troops came for training. Wartime brought a golden age for Northern Irish industry, as shipbuilding and linen-making experienced increased demand.

Early during World War II, the Germans made plans to invade Northern Ireland, but these plans were quickly abandoned because they assumed that Northern Ireland was strategically invulnerable. However, the Germans realized their mistake when they sent 180 planes to drop more than one hundred tons of bombs on Belfast. More than 700 people lost their lives during the bombings of April 14/15. Southern Ireland couldn't simply watch the suffering of their neighbors, and fire brigades from Dublin rushed to help Belfast. Éire even opened refuge centers for the people who lost their houses and businesses in the bombing. On May 4, the Germans returned to destroy the Belfast harbor facilities, killing over 140 people in the process.

Southern Ireland proclaimed its neutrality as early as September 1939, and the northerners resented them for it. However, Éire was a young country, and its leaders were aware that involvement in such a large war could bring down their newly acquired independence. They had to stay out of the war. But that didn't mean Ireland didn't care. Although the government pushed the policies of diplomatic neutrality, privately, the same government carried out secret intelligence and strategic contact with the United Kingdom and the United States. By 1940, the British fared badly in the war, and its government contemplated offering the support of Irish unification in exchange for Éire's involvement. But the diplomatic dialog hurled into a dead-end when Churchill's demand for the reoccupation of the Irish ports was declined. But Dublin continued to carry out espionage activity. In fact, spying on Germans became the most sought occupation at the time, and even the common people were involved (although their activity was limited to contacting illegal IRA members).

On May 30, 1941, the Germans were led astray by jammed radio signals, and they dropped their bombs on Dublin instead of on their Northern Ireland targets. Thirty-four people lost their lives, but this was the only incident that brought Éire in direct contact with the war. Aside from that, the country suffered food shortages and fuel rations. There were only a few automobiles on the streets of Dublin since no one could afford gasoline. But the countryside was busy expanding their tillages and producing enough potatoes to meet the demands of wartime. When the United States joined the war in 1941, Irish neutrality became very loose. Allied airplanes started violating Irish airspace, but the government didn't object. Thousands of civilians decided to join the war at that point, and Éire's government didn't stand in their way. Éire remained officially neutral during the entirety of the war and was closed-off from the events that shaped the future of Europe. Because Éire claimed sovereignty across the whole island, it protested the presence of US troops in Northern Ireland. De Valera refused to close German and Italian diplomatic ministries, and Churchill continuously taunted Ireland for not joining the Allies.

The end of the war brought new determination in both Irelands to leave the economic and social conditions of the pre-war period behind them. They needed to focus their efforts on creating a new, prosperous society. Northern Ireland started this during the war by opening the ministry of health and local governments in 1944. In Éire, the end of the war brought the opportunity to shape the country in the way that has always been in the people's dreams: it was time to create the republic.

The Republic

The Irish political scene in 1945 was dominated by discontent. Rioting and supply shortages continued after the war, and inflation loomed. Farm laborers, industrial workers, and schoolteachers were often on strike, despite the creation of the Labour Court in 1946, which was supposed to deal with disputes between employers and employees. Poverty remained endemic throughout the country, and housing at large was substandard. Emigration continued, and Éire was losing more and more people to it. The one bright spot was that in 1946, electricity was introduced in villages and small isolated family farms. However, it would take the next thirty years for the government to finish the process of electrification of the whole country. Fianna Fáil had already been in power for sixteen years, and the experience it gathered in governing made the party almost abandon its previous political ideals, but the people yearned for a change. Small parties started popping out and proliferating. One such was Clann na Poblachta, founded in July of 1946. Its leader was Seán MacBride (1904–88), an ultra-republican and opponent of the treaty. He was the chief of staff for the IRA, and he brought a powerful IRA presence to the inner circle of the party.

In the first post-war elections of 1948, Clann na Poblachta won 13 percent of the vote, which gave the party ten seats in Parliament. Fianna Fáil remained the largest party; it lost eight seats, which meant it would have to form a coalition. For the first time, a multiparty government was assembled in Ireland, and it included Fine Gael, Clann na Poblachta, and other smaller parties. John A. Costello (1891–1976), who had previously served as attorney general for the Free State, was appointed prime minister. The new government didn't necessarily have previously established common policies, and it was held together only because it shared animosity towards Fianna Fáil. Although de Valera and Fianna Fáil's goal was complete dissociation from Great Britain, it would be this collision that would achieve it. In 1948, the statue of Queen Victoria was removed from the courtyard of Leinster House, the seat of the Irish Parliament, and it marked a symbolic gesture of abandoning the government's ties with London. On September 7, Costello announced that Éire was on the path to leave the commonwealth and become a republic. On December 21, 1948, the Dáil voted and passed the Republic of Ireland Act. Éire formally became a republic on April 18, 1949.

The new government managed to achieve it because, for them, severing the last links to London was more important than the unification of Ireland. The responsibility of Ireland's partition now lay solely on the United Kingdom, and it was their responsibility to unite it again. But London refused to do that when on June 2, 1949, the Parliament at Westminster acknowledged the end of British dominion of Éire but affirmed that Northern Ireland was to remain part of the United Kingdom. The Parliament of Northern Ireland did not give its concession to such a deal. Because the UK decided to cling to Northern Ireland, the Republic of Ireland refused to join the North Atlantic Treaty Organization (NATO), a post-war defense alliance of the West. But the republic did join other European organizations, including the Council of Europe, even though it had to do so alongside Britain. Ireland was unable to join the United Nations (UN), although it applied in 1945; it was vetoed by the Soviet Union as an anti-communist nation, heavily influenced by the Catholic Church. But when a cold war broke out between the US and the Soviet Union in 1955, Ireland was finally accepted into the UN.

During the 1950s and 1960s, Fianna Fáil again came to dominate the politics of the Republic of Ireland, with de Valera creating the government in 1951 and 1957 and Seán Lemass (1899-1971), another leader of the Fianna Fáil, in 1959, 1961, and 1965. Fine Gael revived during the 1960 and continued its conservative politics, but Clann na Poblachta faded, and the Labor Party struggled to inspire people's support. But no political party advocated socialism in predominantly Catholic and conservative Ireland. The major differences between the policies of leading parties were based on their past activities during the civil war. Fianna Fáil remained unwaveringly republican, while Fine Gael was leaning towards more moderate views on government. But Fianna Fáil proved to be a more dynamic political party, and it managed to win more than fifty seats in Parliament in most elections between 1932 and 1977. It appealed to all social classes— workers as well as businessmen and small farmers.

The new Republic of Ireland retained its commercial links to Britain, mainly through trade. After finally achieving the republic, Ireland moved away from economic nationalism and applied for the Marshall Plan, the US program of financial assistance to war-torn Europe. This plan was in place from 1947 until 1952, and Ireland alone received approximately 150 million US dollars in loans and grants. By accepting this aid, the government of Ireland was forced to admit that its previous economic plans yielded low output and productivity rates. It also had to examine its relations with other European countries more closely and admit economic dependency on the British market. The government finally realized that its advocacy of idealistic countryside life was not going to economically sustain the republic.

Emigration continued after the war, with more than half a million people leaving Ireland between 1951 and 1961, mainly for Britain. The population fell to a scant 2.8 million, and the government needed to act quickly to stop emigration. In the 1950s, Southern Ireland looked almost the same as during the 1920s. Barely any rural household had running water and indoor toilets. Modern appliances and central heating were luxuries that only the rich could afford. Even the state infrastructure suffered. The roads were few and were strained by the growing number of vehicles. The society of Ireland was stagnant, conservative, and poor. During the 1950s, the government started a new program, one designed to attract foreign investment. By the middle of the decade, all political parties adopted this program and promoted it. Foreign firms were offered tax breaks and subsidies, and more than 300 companies entered the Irish economy, mainly from the United States. Ireland also joined the World Bank and got access to the International Monetary

Fund. Agriculture was still encouraged, but only its profitable sectors. Farmers were educated in scientifically-advanced techniques during the 1960s, which increased agricultural output significantly. The council for economic and industrial affairs undertook extensive research and introduced modern models of business management and marketing to Ireland. In the second part of the 1960s and throughout the 1970s, Ireland boomed. Annual growth rates averaged 4 percent, which was more than double the pre-war period.

Urbanization and capital-intensive, export-oriented industries expanded. Young people moved to the cities, where opportunities for employment and economic growth were vast. But the rural communities paid the price, and some of the villages completely disappeared. Emigration continued, but it slowed down, allowing the general population of Ireland to grow. By 1971, the demographic had increased more than 100,000 since the Great Famine. The economic gap between the industrial north and the agricultural south started narrowing, which brought many hopes for the possible unification of the two Irelands. But not everything was rosy. Unemployment and inflation rates remained high, and the agricultural growth rate lagged because traditional domestic industries failed to expand. The farming sector was losing the predominant status it had during pre-war Ireland. But educational opportunities expanded during the 1960s as national spending increased and post-primary education was made free. The government also increased children's allowances and occupational benefits. The state pension was introduced, and a Social Welfare Act of 1950 put national healthcare in place as well as unemployment insurance and schemes for widows and orphans.

In June of 1963, US President John F. Kennedy visited Ireland. The whole nation celebrated America's first Catholic president of purely Irish descent. All four of his grandparents were children of Irish emigrants, and Kennedy himself could trace his roots all the way to County Wexford and the Dál gCais people of Thomond. He brought hope to Ireland that the country could advance, just as its emigrants had prospered in the new land. When television was introduced into Irish homes during 1961 and 1962, it symbolized the start of the consumer society that replaced the old conservative one. The broadcasts and access to information changed people's values and helped the country break out of its insular outlook. But this meant that Church officials now had to confront the social and cultural changes that followed technological progress. The Catholic Church's influence in Irish politics and society remained significant, but it was starting to wain. Whenever the church attempted to meddle in the legislative process, the government proved resistant. In such a manner, the Irish pubs won the license to remain open until 11:30 p.m. during weekends, despite the church's harsh objections.

Although the Catholic Church was losing its grasp on society, society remained predominantly—and even increasingly—Catholic. The numbers of Protestants were continuously dropping, and in 1970, they made up only 7 percent of the total population of the republic. This drop in the Protestant population was not due to emigration. The main culprits were increasingly popular intermarriages. Even though the Catholic society of Ireland changed dramatically and showed its capacity for tolerance (and even love) for its Protestant countrymen, the north remained unimpressed. There, the Protestants remained set in their old ways of thinking that unification would only bring Catholic rule under the strict guidance of intolerant papacy, and they were resolved to resist the possibility of unification.

Chapter 10 – The Contemporary History of Ireland

Loyalist banner and the destruction during the Troubles

https://en.wikipedia.org/wiki/The_Troubles#/media/File:Shankilltroubles.jpg

Northern Ireland remained profoundly divided between the sectarian organizations of Protestants and Catholics. The majority of the population in the north were Protestants, and they proudly displayed their might in front of the Catholic residential areas in a yearly parade of the Apprentice Boys of Derry, a Protestant fraternal society. Tensions were always high in Northern Ireland, but the parade organized on August 12, 1969, spurred three-day-long violence that surprised everyone. All the frustrations, injustices, and prejudices that the north had bottled up for generations suddenly burst forth, and the fury of death and destruction followed. The urban centers of Northern Ireland were transformed into battlefields. Civil authorities were unable to cope as the violence overwhelmed them. The British army had to step in to restore order, but instead of being peacemakers, they were made targets of the guerilla wars. Soon, the conflict became a part of everyday life, which had to continue. The people were forced to go on with their business amidst the roadblocks, checkpoints, and constant threat of violent attacks.

The world was watching as Ireland was going through the period of the so-called "Troubles," which lasted approximately thirty years, from the late 1960s to the late 1990s. They were a testament to everything that could go wrong if intolerance was treasured for so long. The Republic of Ireland, although sympathetic to the Catholic minority in the north, rejected the violence of the Provisional IRA. The government abandoned the pursuit of reunification and started new negotiations that would bring satisfaction to both Irish governments. Aside from actively searching for a solution to the troubles in the north, Southern Ireland focused its efforts on gathering wealth. The economy of the Republic spiraled upwards during the progressive 1970s, but the 80s brought a sudden fall. However, during the 1990s, Ireland saw renewed economic growth that excelled all expectations. By the end of the 20th century, the Republic of Ireland had transformed from a backward agricultural society into a modern role model for the nations. The people pulled away from the tragedies of the past and started looking to the future. The social and economic change made the south a prosperous place to live in. Instead of losing its population to emigration, the Republic of Ireland started receiving emigrants from all around the world.

Violence in the North

Even before the events of August 12, 1969, the tensions in Northern Ireland were building for months as the Protestants prepared for their parade to commemorate the Siege of Derry (now Londonderry) in 1689. A Protestant stronghold at the time, Derry was attacked by Catholic King James II and his army, but thirteen apprentice boys shut the city's gates before the ensuing army, and the siege began. Even today, the fraternity Apprentice Boys of Derry symbolically closes the city gates to commemorate the event. Unlike in 1969, today's events are peaceful and tolerant. It is unclear who first started the violence on August 12, but the parade was stopped at the Catholic residential area of Londonderry, the Bogside. There, a road blockade was erected, and when the Apprentice Boys tried to storm the blockade, the Catholics hurled gasoline bombs and stones at them. The violence engulfed the city for three days and even spread to Belfast, where homes on Catholic Falls Road and the Protestant Shankill Road were burned, and gunfire was exchanged. The Royal Ulster Constabulary (RUC) responded by deploying armored cars with mounted guns to drive back the Catholic nationalists. The government mobilized the B-Specials, who overran the Catholic residential area, burning the houses and businesses. However, they only managed to inflame the Catholic community further, and the nationalists rose in retaliation.

The RUC was soon overwhelmed by the mayhem they caused, and they appealed for the reinforcement only the British army could provide. On August 15, an action code-named Operation Banner was launched when the British troops arrived and tried to separate the fighting loyalists (Protestants) and nationalists (Catholics). The Catholics first welcomed the intervention of the army because the UK government issued the Downing Street Declaration on August 19, by which equality and freedom from discrimination were affirmed for both Catholics and Protestants. The government was willing to implement changes and meet most of the demands of the Catholic minority, such as the end of public employment discrimination and the redraw of electoral boundaries. In December, the Ulster Defence Regiment (UDR) was set up to replace the sectarian B-Specials. The UDR was a security force under the control of the British Army, and the Catholics hoped they would be allowed to join its ranks. But their hopes were in vain: in 1970, UDR became a de facto Protestant military force.

But no matter what the government did, the unleashed frustrations of the people continued to cause violence. The residents of Belfast started drawing graffiti on the walls of Catholic houses, which only served to taunt its residents. IRA was almost completely absent from the August disturbances, and the loyalists mocked this republican organization by interpreting IRA as "I Ran Away." The leaders of the IRA sought a response, and on January 11, 1970, they met at a convention in Dublin, where they split into two groups: the Official IRA and the Provisional IRA. The first one wanted to continue fighting for change through official parliamentary means, while the second one committed itself to reunify Ireland by force. The Sinn Féin political party also split, both in the south and in the north, into the official and provisional wings.

The Catholics' hope that the British Army would manage to ensure peace fell apart when that same army started late-night searches of Catholic homes. They were looking for arms, but they were welcomed by gasoline bombs and makeshift weapons. The residents of the Catholic areas of the cities regarded army patrols as further attempts of the Protestants to humiliate them and destroy their property. The British Army was now seen as a faction that sided completely with the Protestants, and riotings renewed by the spring of 1970. The Provisional IRA entered Belfast in late June and joined the fight.

The political forces of Northern Ireland worked to avert further deterioration of the situation. Prime Minister Brian Faulkner (1921-77) and his Unionist Party supported a moderate line despite the continuation of unrest. Protestants and Catholics who sought to reach a compromise united to form the Alliance Party in April of 1970. Moderate Catholic MPs formed a Social Democratic and Labor Party (SDLP) in August and sought the unification of Ireland by consent. They wanted to use official, parliamentary ways to achieve unification, and they renounced violence. At the same time, political bodies who sought to increase division appeared. The Democratic Unionist Party (DUP) was established in September 1971, and it was committed to upholding Protestant dominance in the north. The Ulster Vanguard Movement that sought Ulster's separation was founded in February of 1972.

When the IRA killed the first British soldier in Belfast on February 6, 1971, the bombings multiplied. The Protestant groups answered the attacks with attacks. But the violence was not enough to contain the Catholics, and the unionists started pressuring the government to adopt firmer measures. In August 1971, Faulkner approved the internment of the suspected IRA members for an indefinite period. More than 300 people were arrested and not given the opportunity to defend themselves by trial. But this only served to further antagonize the Catholics, who noticed that all the arrested individuals came from their lines and were badly mistreated. They staged demonstrations across Northern Ireland, and even the moderate Catholics pulled out of public offices. On January 30, 1972, the British army shot thirteen individuals. The day is remembered as "Bloody Sunday," and it caused the resentment of the nationalists. This resentment spilled over to the sister country, and the British embassy in Dublin was burned down on February 2, 1973.

Faulkner's government was unable to deal with the crisis, and London started criticizing and putting pressure on it. By March 1972, London suspended the Northern Irish government and abolished its Parliament, replacing it with the direct rule of Westminster. The British government had to open a new office, secretary of state for Northern Ireland, headed by William Whitelaw (1918-99). But all these changes the British government introduced failed to change the minds of the people that better days were coming. The IRA continued bombing, and on July 21, 1972, nine people were killed in a massacre remembered as "Bloody Friday." The public was shocked by the event, and the violence slowly subsided. However, the year would end with 472 people lost to violent outbursts around Northern Ireland. Although the intensity of the conflict dropped, the violence spread outside the borders of Northern Ireland. In 1973, it even reached London when two cars were rigged with bombs. The explosions killed two individuals and injured around 180 people.

The British government worked on an agreement that would be accepted by both SDLP and Faulkner's Ulster Unionist Party. The SDLP was promised the opening of institutions that would extend over the border and work to connect the two Irelands, while the Unionist Party was promised Northern Ireland would remain part of the United Kingdom. By June 1973, both the SDLP and UUP won a majority, and a new parliament was founded with seventy-eight seats. By November, a joint administration was created, and in December, a Council of Ireland was founded with the task of overseeing matters of common interests between the two Irelands. The new Parliament was again headed by Faulkner, but Gerard Fitt (1926-2005), leader of SDLP, was his deputy.

But cooperation between the two political parties didn't end the conflict. The IRA was unimpressed by the politics and continued launching attacks. Other, more radical political parties opposed the collaboration, and Faulkner was repudiated by the majority of his own MPs, even those who were sitting in Westminster. The voters of both nationalists and loyalists were unsure what the Council of Ireland's role would be, especially the loyalists, who thought that the Council was a step towards the unification of Ireland. On May 28, 1974, Faulkner resigned because he was unable to gather the support of the people for further collaboration. No matter the efforts of the political parties of both Protestants and Catholics, the people were not ready to make a compromise. Irritated by the constant failures to make a difference on a political level, the British government decided to retreat and leave Northern Ireland's politicians to deal with the conflicts on their own. In 1975, efforts to establish cooperation were renewed. But, just as before, they failed to move the people, and negotiations fell apart. The Protestants demanded the return of majority rule, just as it was since the division of Ireland.

Just as politics entered a stalemate, so did the conflict. The killings and violence continued through the rest of the 1970s but slowly subsided in the 1980s, never completely stopping. Deaths dropped from around 300 deaths annually to around eighty. Even though the conflicts were largely contained in Northern Ireland, the Republic suffered, too. In July of 1976, UK ambassador Christopher Ewart-Biggs and a civil servant were killed at Sandyford, Dublin County. The tragedies were numerous, but when an IRA soldier drove a stolen car into the sidewalk and killed three children, a peace movement in Northern Ireland was organized. It was headed by Mairead Corrigan (born 1944), the aunt of the three children, and Betty Williams (1943–2020). The two women gathered signatures for a petition to end the hostilities in Northern Ireland, and women of both Protestant and Catholic families joined them in their peace march through Belfast. On the day of the funeral of the three tragically-killed children, more than 10,000 women of Belfast gathered to support the peace movement. Unfortunately, the IRA attacked the marches. But that didn't diminish the spirits of Mairead Corrigan and Betty Williams. The next peace march gathered around 35,000 people, and this time, people of both genders and religions joined to support peace. Their peace organization believed that violence could be stopped only by education, and they published a biweekly newspaper named *Peace by Peace*. In 1977, both Mairead Corrigan and Betty Williams received a Nobel Peace Prize for their efforts during the previous year. But the violence continued. In 1979, eighteen British soldiers were killed by the IRA, and Earl Mountbatten of Burma was assassinated.

The whole world watched as Northern Ireland burned in conflict. Gruesome images of the riots and assassinations could be seen on televisions in homes across the country. But the people had to continue living. The uncertainty of the "Trouble" brought an economic crash to Northern Ireland. Investors were discouraged from taking their business into risky areas, and the whole United Kingdom could feel the effects. London's ability to supply regional help to Northern Ireland gradually declined. Many factories were forced to shut down during the 1970s and 1980s, and unemployment leaped to 20 percent. The poverty that ensued prevented many Catholics from emigrating, and their numbers started increasing. In 1961, the Catholics represented 35 percent of the total population, and by 1981, that number rose to 40 percent.

During the early 1980s, the IRA prisoners lost their status as political prisoners and started being treated as common criminals. They began protesting the bad conditions in Irish jails and refused to put on the prison uniforms. They also started hunger strikes, and several of the leading IRA figures died of hunger, which served to make them martyrs in the eyes of the Catholic population. The IRA started gaining support not only among the republicans and nationalists of Northern Ireland but also abroad. Demonstrations in their support were organized even in the United States, which made the moderate Catholics of the SDLP anxious to undermine the

IRA's growing support. They turned to the government of Ireland and Great Britain, asking to resume their efforts to establish a power-sharing arrangement for Northern Ireland. The Irish government responded by establishing the New Ireland Forum in 1983, which gathered major parties of the Republic of Ireland and members of SDLP to come up with a common approach to the problem in the north. By 1984, the Forum came up with a set of options that included the union of thirty-two counties in the Irish State: a federal government with islandwide powers, a joint Republic of Ireland, and UK authorities in Northern Ireland. But all their proposals were rejected by the UK government and the Ulster unionists. Nevertheless, the Forum was successful in bringing the Republic of Ireland into the search for the solution to the troubles in Northern Ireland.

The British government under Margaret Thatcher (1925-2013) was, at first, supporting the Ulster unionists and their wish for Protestant dominion over the Catholics. But in time, Thatcher came to realize that Northern Ireland needed to come up with a power-sharing scheme so that the needs of the minority population could be met. In November of 1984, Thatcher and the Irish Prime Minister Garret Fitzgerald (1926-2011) held a summit, and together they issued a call for respect for both communities in Northern Ireland. The product of the meeting of the two prime ministers was the Anglo-Irish Hillsborough Agreement, signed in 1985. This agreement put in motion a mechanism for the joint reaction of both governments, the UK and the Republic of Ireland, to the specific crises in Northern Ireland. Both the UK and the Republic of Ireland affirmed that the status of the north wouldn't change without the concession of the majority of its population. The British-Irish Intergovernmental Center was established, and they met regularly in the forums to discuss the trouble in Northern Ireland.

The Republic Progress

While the conflict in Northern Ireland raged, the citizens and the government of the Republic of Ireland could only watch. They resented the violence that engulfed the northern half of their island, and they set goals for themselves to focus on growing their nation and its economy. Only through prosperity would the Republic be able to help the Irish people who suffered in the Troubles. The Second Program for Economic Expansion was launched in 1964, and the third started in 1970. They were ambitious programs designed to launch the Republic's economy forward, and their main goals were to attract foreign investors and promote the export of manufactured goods. Regional free trade became the priority, and the prospects of the country's economy improved even more when the Republic of Ireland joined the European Economic Community (EEC) on January 1, 1973. Foreign investors were now even more attracted to opening their businesses in the Republic, and the first companies that produced electronics, chemicals, and home appliances took up residence in Ireland. They helped greatly in diversifying the country's export market. The economy grew at a steady 4 percent rate yearly, except during 1973-74 and 1979, when energy prices skyrocket across the whole Western world.

The political parties that were overlooking the economic changes of the country were still the same. Fianna Fáil, Fine Gael, and the Labour Party still dominated the political scene, but the political regime of the country changed very often—five times from 1966 to 1982. Observing the violence that grasped the north, these political parties gradually moved away from their radical policies. New leaders took over, and the parties were, in general, better managed and had access to more funds. But the government of a country that progresses so quickly has its turmoils, too, and the Republic didn't go unaffected by the events in the north. In April of 1970, a scandal almost overthrew the government when a shipment of arms heading from the continent to Northern Ireland was found by customs officials of the Dublin airport. Two ministers who were believed to be involved in the incident were immediately dismissed: Charles Haughey, Minister for Finance, and Neil Blaney, Minister for Agriculture and Fisheries.

In June 1981, the Republic of Ireland elected a new government, with Dr. Garret FitzGerald heading it as prime minister. His priority was to address the effects of the economic crises of 1973-74 and 1979. Since, in that period, Ireland had been hit by two oil crises, bank strikes, and pay raises for public employees, the previous prime ministers had increased the national debt. When economic woes lingered, the debt piled up, and Fitzgerald had to deal with it. The economy dominated his government's politics throughout the 1980s, but all the measures proposed by the government were defeated in voting. One of them was for budget cuts in 1981, and the other was a tax increase, which was defeated in 1982. The recession continued.

The social change that started with the foundation of the Republic of Ireland continued despite its economic troubles. The transformation of Irish society is best presented through demographics. From 2.8 million in 1961, the population jumped to 3.4 million in only twenty years. The country managed to reverse the decline due to immigration, and the population not only grew but also became younger. By 1980, almost half of the people were younger than twenty-five, and the government secured them access to higher education. Throughout the 1970s, the education system was changed to include a new curriculum, and the government built larger and better-equipped schools. Besides the state-run universities founded in 1968, regional technical colleges were established. Modernization was seen everywhere—from schools to hospitals, public offices, and even private homes. With it, a better standard of life came to Ireland, though not for everyone. Around 20 percent of the population still endured poverty, and in the urban areas, crime rates increased, especially in Dublin. The rising population also meant more young people were becoming the workforce of very limited industries. This led to severe competition for available jobs, and unemployment rates started increasing. Industrial expansion also introduced a new worry to the population and the government of Ireland: pollution.

The economic woes of Ireland continued through the 1980s and into the early 1990s, and emigration rates started rising again. More than 50,000 people were leaving the island yearly, sparking the fear that the demographic patterns of the Great Famine were returning. The national debt reached an incredible 94.5 percent of gross domestic production (GDP) by 1993. But even then, changes in the domestic economy could be seen. Between 1987 and 1992, the gross national product (GNP) grew 30 percent, and the economy started expanding by 2 percent a year. Unemployment started dropping as the new, highly-educated generation entered the workforce, and the demand for opening new industries grew. Unemployment fell to 7.7 percent by 1998, and then to 3.8 in 2000. By the end of the 20th century, the inflation rate fell to 2.4 percent, down from 9 percent between 1995 and 1999. The living standard in Ireland at the end of the century caught up with the rest of Western Europe.

Many factors, both domestic and foreign, are to be thanked for this economic turnaround in Ireland. The government introduced a campaign by which it managed to target and attract high-tech companies to come and open their businesses in Ireland. Major international computer firms established their presence on the island, attracted by low wages and the government's tax cuts for businesses. Ireland could offer a highly-sought young, educated, English-speaking workforce, and the island's geographic location and time zone made it a perfect location for the firms that did business with the Western world. Because of its membership in EEC, Ireland gained access to Europe's ever-growing market when, in 1993, European Union was created.

The population of Ireland remained largely influenced by the Catholic Church, even though the institution's power to influence politics was reduced. Abortion remained illegal in Ireland when the Eight Amendment entered the constitution in 1983. By this amendment, the unborn fetus had the same value as its mother; however, Parliament gained the right to decide on abortion legality. In 2013, the Irish Parliament voted that abortion could be performed in the country if it was done to save the life of a woman. This law was introduced after a scandal from the previous year when a woman died because she was denied an abortion even though she had suffered a septic miscarriage. This incident sparked many women's movements, and the discussion on this topic was introduced to the Citizens' Assembly in 1916-17. Abortion was finally legalized in 2018. Women's activist movements were alive in Ireland throughout the 1970s and 1980s as they fought for their rights to enter the workforce and to receive pay equal to that of men. The impact of modern-day globalization changed the value system of Irish society. The country started linking itself with the trends and perspective characteristic of the modern Western world. Other social changes came with the improved economic status of the country. Society's tendency to open-mindedness and vision to the future first brought decriminalization of homosexuality in adults in 1993, and in 1995, divorce was finally legalized. Contraceptives, banned since 1935, were now entering the country freely and were available to everyone who needed them. The Catholic Church started softening its definitive opinions and was pushed to the margins during morality debates.

End of Violence

In 1985, when the Republic of Ireland joined the search for the end of the conflict in the north, it immediately set up an International Fund for Ireland to provide money for the regional development of Ulster and the areas of Northern Ireland that bordered the Republic. The hope was that the violence would stop if the citizens had better economic prospects. Even the elections of 1987 showed a change in the political opinion of the people, as the moderate SDLP's share in the vote rose. But the violence didn't stop; it didn't even decline. In the year of the election, eight IRA men were killed in an attack on the County Armagh police station, while eleven civilians died and sixty-three were injured by a bomb the IRA members set at Enniskillen.

The Republic government continued to fight the violence with specific measures designed to appease the people. Similar to its plan to increase living standards for its own citizens, the government tried to address unemployment issues in Northern Ireland. In 1990, the Northern Ireland Fair Employment Act was issued, and the Fair Employment Commission was created to guarantee that Catholics would get a fair share of jobs. But it was not enough to stop the conflicts. A change in general opinion was evident, as people's support for the IRA and Sinn Féin declined, but the radicals were determined to reach their goal by using force. In 1992, thirty-six civilians and thirty-nine unionists were killed. Police strove to subdue the violence wherever it popped up, but the loyalists saw those actions as a sign that the police were encouraging compromise. Friction between the RUC and the loyalists rose, which led to the dissolution and banning of the Ulster Defence Association in 1992.

On December 15, 1993, prime ministers John Major (UK) and Albert Reynolds (Ireland) issued a joint Downing Street Declaration by which they affirmed that it was up to the people of Northern Ireland to exercise their right to self-determination and that if it was the will of the people, Northern and Southern Ireland would unite. The declaration gave the right to all the people of Northern Ireland, regardless of their religious or political stance, to decide the fate of the country. Both the governments of the UK and the Republic of Ireland would continue to search for a constitutional means to end the violence, and even radical parties such as Sinn Féin could join the talks if they abandoned the violence. Since London showed through the declaration that it had no reason or will to keep its presence in Northern Ireland, the IRA lost the reason that justified its use of violence. The declaration opened the door to moving ahead, and the people grasped the opportunity.

President of the United States, William J. Clinton, approved a visa for the leader of the Sinn Féin, Gerry Adams, who was involved in gathering the support of the American-Irish for the republican cause. The British objected since Sinn Féin was a radical party, and they thought Clinton was openly supporting it. But the US president conditioned Adams, pressuring him to abandon the violent politics he was leading until now. This pressure was felt strongly even in Ireland, and in August 1994, the IRA agreed to a ceasefire. On October 13, a Protestant paramilitary organization, Combined Loyalist Military Command, announced a ceasefire as well. The break in the violence gave both the British and Irish governments the chance to enter into dialogue with radical groups such as the Ulster Democratic Party, the Progressive Unionist Party, and Sinn Féin. In 1995, the UK and Irish governments published proposals for constitutional settlement under the name *A New Framework Agreement*. This document sketched the details of the new political structure in Northern Ireland, relations between Northern and Southern Ireland, and the degree of UK involvement.

In 1995, the US pledged to increase its support to the International Fund for Ireland, and ex-Senator George Mitchell was appointed the special ambassador tasked with dealing with Northern Ireland's conflict. Gerry Adams received an unlimited visa so he could join the talks in Washington DC. But the British government announced it would continue the talks with Sinn Féin only when the IRA agreed to decommission its weapons. Nevertheless, the initiatives by various governments moved ahead, and it seemed that everyone was eager to come to a solution to the violence in Northern Ireland. But among the people, the support for sectarian separatism grew. Some of the politicians even maintained the sentiment for violence. In 1995, Gerry Adams held a rally of republicans in which he promised that the IRA would not go away. In the same year, the Orange Order's marches produced outbursts of violence in Belfast and Portadown.

When, in 1996, the International Body on Decommissioning of Weapons urged all parties of Northern Ireland to give up their weapons as a symbol of commitment to non-violent methods, the IRA defied and ended the ceasefire. In February and June, massive bomb detonations shook London and Manchester. The violence renewed, and it continued through 1997. The Orange Order parades continued to spark violence from rioting Catholics in Portadown. In Belfast, parade routes were drafted so that the unionists would intentionally march through Catholic neighborhoods and taunt them. The violence during the parades and marches of Protestants became so gruesome that, in 1998, a Northern Ireland Parades Commission was set up, and it held the power to ban, reroute, or restrict parades in any way.

In May of 1997, in Britain, the Labour Party won under the leadership of Prime Minister Tony Blair. The new secretary of state for Northern Ireland was also elected, Marjorie "Mo" Mowlam (1949–2005), and she announced that the decommission of weapons would no longer halt all-party talks. But to continue the dialog and push ahead with the settlement, the IRA had to reinstate the ceasefire. The IRA complied, and on September 9, Sinn Féin joined the peace talks. The next fall and winter saw intensive negotiations on three levels: between London and Dublin, Belfast and Dublin, and among the political parties of Northern Ireland. The deadline for completion of the agreement was set for midnight on April 9, 1998. The result was not a peace settlement but a "Good Friday Agreement" (alternatively known as the Belfast Agreement), a sixty-five-page document with the vehicle of peace in motion. The framework of the new government was laid out, but the political parties also agreed to declare their commitment to nonviolence, partnership, mutual respect, and equality. Two new administrative bodies were set up: the North-South Ministerial Council and the British-Irish Council. Their task was to consult the new government on issues of regional importance.

The central points of the Good Friday Agreement were the confirmation that no constitutional changes could be made unless approved by the people, the decommissioning of the weapons by paramilitary organizations, the reconstruction of the Northern Irish police, and the release of all political prisoners. The referendum was set in both Northern and Southern Ireland to estimate the support for the agreement among the population. The results showed that the south fully supported the agreement, and so did the north, but to a lesser extent. Northern Ireland voted yes to the agreement by 71.12 percent, while in the south, that percentage was 94.39.

The Northern Ireland Assembly elections were held on June 25, 1998, and the Ulster Unionist Party won a majority with twenty-eight seats. The DUP won twenty, the SDLP twenty-four, Sinn Féin eighteen, and other smaller parties collectively won eighteen. The assembly met on July 1 and elected David Trimble as the first minister-designate for the Northern Ireland Executive, a body designed to implement the policies of the Good Friday Agreement. John Hume, leader of SDLP, and David Trimble won the Nobel Peace Prize in 1998 for their efforts to bring peace to Northern Ireland.

Several months after the Good Friday Agreement was accepted and the Northern Ireland Executive was set up, violence resumed. The abandoning of old habits proved difficult, and the unionists bombed a Catholic house, killing three brothers, ages eight to ten. On August 15, the "Real IRA" retaliated by setting a fifty-pound bomb in a parked car near a shopping street in Omagh. The explosion killed twenty-nine civilians and injured around 200 people. Sinn Féin had clearly failed to decommission the IRA, and the government formation failed. But, in 1999, the Northern Ireland Assembly was in session, ending the decade with insecure peace. Optimism returned, and the parties started cooperating again to bring permanent peace to Northern Ireland.

Conclusion

The Ireland of the 21st century little resembles the old country. Today, Ireland enjoys one of the world's healthiest and wealthiest economies. The population started growing exponentially in 2008, and it continues even today. The country whose modern history was defined by violence, poverty, and emigration made the greatest turnaround in the history of Europe's civilization. Ireland today draws immigrants from all over the world with the most stable economy in Europe and further. But the society of Ireland remains conservative to a degree. The Catholic Church still bears a significant influence on the country's society and politics. However, signs of progress are everywhere, and even the Church has started loosening its conservative grasp on the island.

The Emerald Island stays divided—politically, religiously, and culturally. The bonds between Northern Ireland, the Republic of Ireland, and the United Kingdom are complex even today, but the focus is no longer on violence and hatred. It has shifted to mutual respect, understanding, and cooperation. Recent prospects on both economic and social levels are bringing new outlooks to Ireland that are serving to push the country forwards. People no longer dwell on the conflicts of the past and are willing to join their forces to move their country into a better future. Even though divided, Ireland is united in its spirit and its willingness to prospect. But tensions and violence still ensue during the Protestant parades in Ulster during the summer. Each year, there is less and less violence. The newer generations are shocked by the hostilities and are willing to forget them. The popular opinion today is a stark contrast to that of only twenty to thirty years ago.

With the end of the conflicts in the north and the spread of Irish emigrants throughout the Western world, the Emerald Island became a romanticized place of rolling green hills, a landscape that sparks the imagination of the many tourists that visit the island today. The old myths and legends are revived and retold to newer generations that are, it seems, able to connect to their ancestors, at least in spirit. Irish people everywhere celebrate St. Patrick's Day, a celebration that has gradually entered other cultures willing to show respect to this proud nation. Some bad stereotypes about Ireland remain, such as that the Irish are violent or that the whole island is backward. But these can't be further from the truth. In the 21st century, Ireland stands as an example to all countries that still suffer civil strife. An island, a country, and a nation able to pull itself out of violence and in only twenty years become one of the strongest economies in Europe deserves we all take a respectful bow to it.

Here's another book by Captivating History that you might like

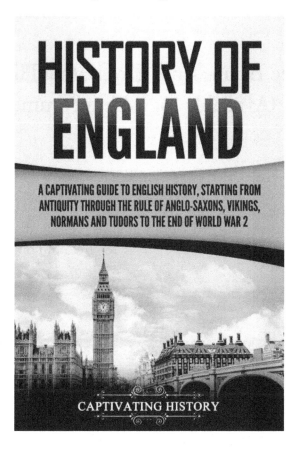

Free Bonus from Captivating History (Available for a Limited time)

Hi History Lovers!

Now you have a chance to join our exclusive history list so you can get your first history ebook for free as well as discounts and a potential to get more history books for free! Simply visit the link below to join.

Captivatinghistory.com/ebook

Also, make sure to follow us on Facebook, Twitter and Youtube by searching for Captivating History.

References

Crawford, E. Margaret. *Famine: the Irish Experience, 900-1900: Subsistence Crises and Famines in Ireland.* John Donald Publishers, 1989.

Cronin, Michael, and Liam OCallaghan. *A History of Ireland.* Palgrave, Macmillan Education, 2015.

Davin, Anna. *Irish History.* Oxford University Press, 1991.

Fitzhugh, William W., and Elisabeth I. Ward. *Vikings: the North Atlantic Saga.* Smithsonian Institution Press, in Association with the National Museum of Natural History, 2000.

Foster, R. F. *The Oxford History of Ireland.* Oxford University Press, 2001.

Moore, Thomas. *History of Ireland.* Forgotten Books, 2015.

Newman, Peter R. *Companion to Irish History, 1603-1921: From the Submission of Tyrone to Partition.* New York: Facts On File, 1991

Norman, Edward Robert., and Edward Robert Norman. *A History of Modern Ireland (1800-1969).* Penguin Books, 1973.

Sykes, Bryan, and Bryan Sykes. *Saxons, Vikings, and Celts: the Genetic Roots of Britain and Ireland.* Norton, 2007.

Thierry, Augustin. *History of the Conquest of England by the Normans: Its Causes, and Its Consequences, in England, Scotland, Ireland, and on the Continent.* Cambridge University Press, 2011.